T0353087

LEMON

ROSEMARY

About the Author

Raechel Henderson is a Pagan and witch following an eclectic and independent path. She currently works with Hestia and Turtle in her magical practice. She contributes articles to Llewellyn's almanacs and calendars, and she blogs about magic, creativity, and living by your own patterns. Raechel is a dual-class seamstress/shieldmaiden and has been sewing professionally since 2008. She is also the author of *Sew Witchy* (Llewellyn, 2018). Raechel lives in Chicago.

the SCENT of

LEMON

&

ROSEMARY

*Working Domestic Magick
with Hestia*

Raechel Henderson

Llewellyn Publications
Woodbury, Minnesota

FIRST EDITION
Fifth Printing, 2024

Cover design by Kevin R. Brown
Interior illustrations by Sara Koncilja

Llewellyn Publications is a registered trademark of Llewellyn Worldwide Ltd.

Library of Congress Cataloging-in-Publication Data
Names: Henderson, Raechel, author.
Title: The scent of lemon & rosemary : working domestic magic with Hestia / Raechel Henderson.
Other titles: Scent of lemon and rosemary
Description: First edition. | Woodbury, Minnesota : Llewellyn Publications, 2021. | Includes bibliographical references. | Summary: "Spells, crafts, and recipes for creating harmonious energy in each room and turning your entire home into a sacred space"—Provided by publisher.
Identifiers: LCCN 2021000472 (print) | LCCN 2021000473 (ebook) | ISBN 9780738766676 (paperback) | ISBN 9780738766881 (ebook)
Subjects: LCSH: Hestia (Greek deity) | Witchcraft. | Magic. | Home—Religious aspects. | Sacred space.
Classification: LCC BF1566 .H46 2021 (print) | LCC BF1566 (ebook) | DDC 133.4/3—dc23
LC record available at https://lccn.loc.gov/2021000472
LC ebook record available at https://lccn.loc.gov/2021000473

Llewellyn Publications
A Division of Llewellyn Worldwide Ltd.
2143 Wooddale Drive
Woodbury, MN 55125-2989
www.llewellyn.com

Printed in the United States of America

Also by Raechel Henderson

Sew Witchy: Tools, Techniques & Projects for Sewing Magick

Contents

Prometheus may have stolen fire for the humans,
but it's Hestia who keeps it alight.

—MELISSA HILL, "IMBOLC INVOCATION TO THE FIRE GODDESSES"

INTRODUCTION

On September 9, 1999, I wrote the following in a spiral-bound notebook: "I have found my goddess teacher: Hestia, that hearth/goddess of fire. It seems appropriate that I learn from a hearth goddess what is needed to prepare for winter." Further down the page I wrote, "By the time I have finished this tablet, I hope to have more rituals to Hestia to put in a Book of Shadows for myself." Spoiler alert: I never wrote that Book of Shadows. I was three years into an abusive relationship that would last another nine. My commitment to my witchcraft and spiritual path often had to take a backseat to navigating that reality.

Even so, Hestia never left my thoughts. I was invested in making a safe place, a home, all those years. Through garden plans and household crafts, recipes and cookery, cleaning schedules and decor, I attempted to change my situation by changing my environment. Throw pillows and goulash can only do so much, however, and even the hardiest weeds cannot grow where there is nothing to nourish them. During those years I would touch upon Hestia, reaching out to her, asking her to help me make things right. But this goddess of hearth and home knew there wasn't a place for her there. Eventually, in 2008, I gained the strength and support I needed to break away from that relationship and start again. When I did so, Hestia was waiting for me.

I didn't formally dedicate myself to her until 2019—twenty years after I first encountered her. I had a lot of emotional fallout to work through, which led me to working with goddesses such as Hecate for several years. Even so, Hestia was there, in the background, keeping the hearth burning as I discovered what kind of person I wanted to be. My relationship with Hestia is more partnership than worship. I ask her to help me in my work, both magickal and mundane. I make offerings to her, in gratitude for her blessings and aid, but when I address her, my language is more familiar than reverent. That informality doesn't make our connection any less meaningful.

At the time when COVID-19 spread across the globe, ripping away people's sense of safety and exposing the weaknesses of various governments, I felt that Hestia was more relevant than ever. I wrote this book during the first half of 2020, during a shelter-in-place order that lasted much longer than anyone had expected. In many places, others experienced the same. We were stuck in homes that we may not have spent much time in before. Work and socializing may have kept us away from our homes for hours each day. For some people, this meant learning new skills: cooking, cleaning, the fine arts of housekeeping, and even new hobbies. For others, this meant being stuck in an unsafe environment for who knew how long. Some folks were dealing with isolation and loneliness. Others were reevaluating just what the home meant to them.

The Scent of Lemon & Rosemary is the collected wisdom from all those years of discreet workings with Hestia, the Greek goddess of the hearth. All the spells and rituals are included, as well as a deep dive into her mythology and meaning in today's society. I've also included several crafts you can make to create a cozy home environment. The book has an unapologetic leftist ideology, as I've found Hestia to be incompatible with capitalism and all it entails.

You don't have to be a polytheist, or any kind of religious, to use the information in this book. The concept of a safe home goes beyond deities. Security and safety land on the second tier of Maslow's hierarchy of needs. You can perform the spells and rituals without worshipping Hestia or even invoking her at all if you wish. You don't have to be Pagan or a witch, even. The crafts, recipes, and advice on housekeeping don't require magick. Much of it is drawn from knowledge our grandparents and ancestors had.

Much of the book relies on an attitude of make-do and of reducing, reusing, and recycling. There is an emphasis on community, as Hestia's influence extended beyond individual households to the societies they built. *The Scent of Lemon & Rosemary* very much recognizes that "it takes a village" and that the integrity of that village rests on how safe and strong the household is.

Throughout this book, you will find recipes and spells that are aimed at health issues. Nothing in this book is meant to replace the care of a physician or modern medicine. I am a witch, meaning I get my flu shot every year and also charm my depression meds so they will work on the magickal as well as physical plane. No amount of essential oil is going to treat diabetes. So when using the spells and recipes in *The Scent of Lemon & Rosemary*, keep in mind that modern medicine is for treating disease and herbal medicine is for treating symptoms.

While I've written this book to be read from start to finish, I am aware that might not be the way many readers want to approach it. For those who prefer to go directly to the information that interests them, I've tried to organize the book to allow you to do so. The first two chapters introduce you to the two main topics of this book: Hestia and the home. "Hestia: The First and Last" covers the mythology, worship and relevance of Hestia. "The Home: An Anatomy of Comfort" covers the house as a whole and briefly covers what the following chapters dedicated to each room will involve. The "Making Magick" chapter covers various techniques, components and concepts that are used throughout the book and in witchcraft in general. If you are an experienced witch, sections such as "Four Magickal Techniques" might be familiar to you, and you can skip them if you wish. Other sections, such as "Materia Magica," relate specifically to the spells and practices in this book. The three chapters "Breaking Bread," "Cleaning," and "Creating Your Own Wheel of the Year" cover tasks and activities that are not room or Hestia specific. The chapter "Modern Values" expands the lens to explore our lives in the context of Hestia, the home, and Paganism.

However you approach this book—as a Pagan, a witch, a homekeeper, or any mix of the three—you will find the contents useful. Thank you for reading *The Scent of Lemon & Rosemary*. May love and happiness always dwell in your home.

1

HESTIA: THE FIRST AND LAST

Hestia, according to Greek mythology, was the oldest child of the six children of Kronos and Rhea. Kronos, having been warned that his rule would be overturned by one of his children, did what most subjects of Greek myths do: he attempted to avoid his fate and in so doing ensured it would happen. He swallowed his children as his wife Rhea gave birth to them: first Hestia, then Demeter and Hera, then Poseidon and Hades. When Rhea gave birth to Zeus, she handed Kronos a boulder instead of the newborn. This allowed Zeus to grow up and overthrow Kronos, in the process forcing his father to regurgitate his siblings in reverse order to how they were swallowed. First came Hades, then Poseidon, followed by Hera and then Demeter, and finally Hestia.

This order, being the firstborn and the first down Kronos's gullet and then coming out last, is the reasoning behind her epithet of "first and last."

Beyond the story of her origin, there are only two other Hestian myths. Both of the myths deal with Hestia's marital status and virginity. The second one recounts attempted rape. If you feel you will have difficulties reading about that, you can skip down to the next section on page 8.

"Hymn V: To Aphrodite" explains how Hestia came to be the guardian of the Olympian flame and the reason she is offered the first portion of sacrifices and offerings. Both Apollo and Poseidon wished to marry Hestia. But Hestia "was wholly unwilling, nay, stubbornly refused; and touching the head of father Zeus who holds the aegis, she, that fair goddess, sware a great oath which has in truth been fulfilled, that she would be a maiden all her days." Zeus agreed to this, setting "her place in the midst of the house" and giving her "the richest portion. In all the temples of the gods she has a share of honour, and among all mortal men she is chief of the goddesses."[1]

Ovid relates the second myth regarding Hestia. Hestia was attending a feast with other gods, nymphs, and satyrs. Everyone gets drunk and Hestia ends up passed out on the lawn. Priapus, "the red saviour of gardens," finds Hestia and decides to rape her. As he's getting started, a nearby donkey brays, waking Hestia, and alerting the other guests to what's going on. In response, Priapus is chased off.[2]

Taking those two myths together, one would expect Hestia's sphere of influence to be limited to the household. This wasn't so for ancient Greeks. Hestia was in charge of not only the hearth in the home but also the hearth that was the center of city life.

She was called "goddess of the senate," and a statue and altar to her were part of the senate house of Athens, according to Aeschines. In the same passage, Aeschines writes that senators would swear by Hestia, indicating her connection to the public,

---

1. *Hesiod, the Homeric Hymns, and Homerica*, trans. Hugh G. Evelyn-White (Cambridge, MA: Harvard University Press, 1914), "V: To Aphrodite," lines 24–31.

2. Ovid, *Fasti*, trans. A. J. Boyle and R. D. Woodard (New York: Penguin, 2000), book 6, lines 319–48.

legal life of a city.[3] And in his "Nemean Ode 11," Pindar writes, "Daughter of Rhea, you who have received the town hall under your protection, Hestia, sister of Zeus the highest and of Hera who shares his throne."[4]

This gives us a goddess who bookends all actions. She's the first into the fray, the first to attempt to solve a problem, and the last to leave or give up. She's there throughout, a stable foundation and the center around which all the action revolves. It is her origin, her birth and then rebirth, that sets the stage for Hestia's domain. Stuck in Kronos's stomach, she spends her childhood and youth in one place.

That in one of her only myths Hestia rejects the most traditional role assigned to women, that of wife, and in doing so is set up above all other gods is an interesting departure from the traditional path of Greek goddesses. One could make the cynical argument that Zeus recognized the Olympians needed a housekeeper. But giving her the "richest" portion as well as a share in the honor at the temples of the other gods rebuts that point, I feel. Zeus, a god known for his philandering, misogynistic ways, not only gave his older sister what she wanted, but ensured, through his power as the king of the Olympians, that she would always have charge of her own fate and that everyone—mortal and immortal alike— knew it.

With Greek mythology chockablock full of nonconsensual encounters, it's almost a relief to find a story in which the victim is saved and the would-be rapist stopped. Looking beyond the obvious

---

3. Aeschines, *The Speeches of Aeschines,* trans. Charles Darwin Adams (Cambridge, MA: Harvard University Press, 1919), 193.

4. Pindar, *Nemean Odes,* trans. Diane Arnson Svarlien (Perseus Digital Library, 1990), ode 11, lines 1–5. http://www.perseus.tufts.edu/hopper/text?doc =Perseus%3Atext%3A1999.01.0162%3Abook%3DN.%3Apoem%3D11.

themes of this account, we see a goddess who is secure in her body autonomy. Not only that, others around her recognize her right to her sovereignty. More than that, there's a strong theme of community. Hestia isn't left to fend off Priapus by herself. Once the donkey sounds the alarm, all the gods come rushing to her defense.

Being the family enlarged to encompass a city, culture, or country, the state would, of course, fall under Hestia's influence. It's this association that enforces the idea of social structure. Despite the fact that Hestia eschews the role of wife and maintains her independence, she oversees the order of the house and the state beyond that. Hestia's dominion over home and state enforces the idea that the personal is the political. And for that work, she gets the best portions of the sacrifice.

Ancient Values, Modern Significance

Her domain over the personal and political makes Hestia especially relevant for modern-day Pagans and witches. More than that, however, her significance when it comes to family, self-determination, social justice, anti-capitalism, and the like help give a blueprint for building a worship and magickal practice that encompasses a life that recognizes and tries to address the failings of many modern institutions.

Hestia Is Ancient, Not Old-Fashioned

The concept of family is often presented as immutable, an idea that is the bedrock of society. The truth, however, is that the family "unit" has never been set in stone. Different eras and societies have all envisioned what it means to be family in varying ways. Up until fairly recently, multiple generations and extended family all lived together under one roof. And even today the nuclear family isn't the default. In many cultures grandparents, siblings, aunts and uncles, and their children still live together. As with most things that involve humanity, history is a lot more complex and messier than someone pushing an agenda would want you to think. Spend even five minutes talking to a historian or a sociologist and you discover that the "nuclear family" that is held up as the ideal by conservative people is a modern concept.

All of this is to say that Hestia is not the goddess of one type of family or home. She is not interested in rigid adherence to a particular social structure. In her eyes, the chosen family is just as important and valid as the biological family. And the reason for this is simple: Hestia, the most important goddess to the Greeks, is the goddess of the hearth, which then extends her sovereignty to the state. Her authority, and thus the natural hierarchy, flows from the individual family to the larger organization of the state. Thus, the government has no say in what constitutes a family, only the individuals making up the family can make that call. Family comes first, and then the state, as per her mythology.

To this end, when I talk about family in this book, I am not defining what that family looks like. A lesbian couple with adopted children? Family. A polyamorous group? Family. Friends who live in different cities but call each other family? Family. The makeup of the group is not important; it is the feeling of mutual love, affection, and support that are the factors we take into account.

EXERCISE
Your Family Unit

Consider the following questions: How do you define family? Who is in your family? Who offers you support? Who do you support? Who would you focus on when you work protection spells or when you pray to Hestia? Identifying your family unit before you begin to include them in your spellwork or prayers means you won't be fumbling for names when you are in the middle of a ritual or spell.

Hestia Advocates Self-Rule

There is a term I was introduced to years ago by the book *Hermits: The Insights of Solitude* by Peter France: *idiorhythmic routine.*[5] The term was used in the context of how certain monasteries would allow the monks to organize their days rather than have a set schedule. Thus, idiorhythmic means to live by one's own life patterns. How this relates to Hestia is obvious. The goddess took her life in her own hands (literally placing a hand on Zeus's head).

Hestia highlights the importance of bodily autonomy, self-determination, and living in a way that is true to oneself. Those three priorities can feel out of reach when one lives in a country that tries to control them through actions like passing antiabortion or anti-LGBTQI laws, or how it treats those who are black, Indigenous, and people of color (BIPOC). This is where we turn to her and magick to supplement the mundane-world work we do to build a more equitable society.

And as Hestia is found both in the home and the state, we can work with her on the personal level in structuring our routines around our unique circumstances. For example, I am a night owl. I find I do my best work when everyone else is asleep and have a hard time functioning in the mornings. Currently, I have the luxury of keeping this schedule. That's not always possible, and for a majority of people, work and school hours interfere with having a schedule that follows their internal clock.

In light of the other concepts discussed in this chapter, having a schedule that follows our own internal clock might seem

---

5. Peter France, *Hermits: The Insights of Solitude* (New York: St. Martin's, 1997).

less important. Knowing when you are at your most alert, when you have no other obligations, and even when you feel magickal is useful in scheduling spellwork. There often seems to be a lot of emphasis on proper placement of altars, magickal timing of spells, what tools to have on hand, and so on. But if, when the moon is full and the planets are all aligned, you can't perform the spell because your schedule doesn't allow the time or you're not feeling up to it, all that planning will be for naught. Magick, to be effective, has to be worked. The spell cast at your kitchen sink has a greater chance of working than the one left gathering dust on your altar.

 EXERCISE
Your Idiorhythmic Routine

Consider the following questions: What is a typical day like for you? Are you a night owl or a morning bird, or perhaps even an afternoon pigeon? In an ideal world when you would perform spellwork? Rituals? If you look at your schedule now, where could you fit in those practices? When was the last time you cast a spell? When was the last you weren't able to? What was the obstacle? How could you minimize those obstacles in the future?

Hestia Is a Social Justice Warrior

Hestia, being the goddess of the hearth and state, is also going to have some concern over larger, more intellectual concerns. The rights of all people fall under her purview as a goddess of the state. Families are affected by social justice issues. For example, in the United States, African Americans are incarcerated at a rate of five times more than whites, including being jailed over drug offenses that white people are not.[6] This has a direct and damaging effect on African American families. When Trump took office in 2017, his administration started separating the children of asylum seekers from their families, causing lasting psychological damage to the parents and children.[7] These are just two examples of how injustice on the state level negatively impacts the family.

All of this is not to say that you are expected to be chaining yourself to a bulldozer to protest deforestation. Protest and social change also require support work: people donating time and money to organizations, phone banking, bringing supplies to those protesting, calling and writing to politicians and corporations, abiding by boycotts and strikes, and so on. Not everyone can afford to be arrested at a protest, but there are countless ways you can participate in actions for social justice reform.

EXERCISE
Your Social Justice Class

Consider the following questions: What social justice issues are important to you? What organizations are there that are focused on those issues? How could you support those organizations? What spellwork could you do in service of those organizations or issues?

---

6. Ashley Nellis, "The Color of Justice: Racial and Ethnic Disparity in State Prisons," the Sentencing Project, June 14, 2016, https://www.sentencingproject.org/publications/color-of-justice-racial-and-ethnic-disparity-in-state-prisons/.

7. Hajar Habbach, Kathryn Hampton, and Ranit Mishori, "You Will Never See Your Child Again: The Persistent Psychological Effects of Family Separation," Physicians for Human Rights, February 25, 2020, https://phr.org/our-work/resources/you-will-never-see-your-child-again-the-persistent-psychological-effects-of-family-separation/.

Hestia Is Anti-capitalist

You are going to find a theme of anti-capitalism running through this book. I'll expand on this in the section "No Ethical Consumption under Capitalism" on page 202. Briefly, however, I'll point out here that capitalism is a fairly recent economic system that runs counter to much of what Hestia teaches. She's not going to care about stocks and profit margins. This is not because she is an ancient goddess who has no experience with modern economics, but because Hestia's focus is primarily on the good of the family. If a CEO tells her how much profit their company made, she's going to want to know how many homeless that money housed, how many hungry fed, how many sick treated. As a protector of the state, she isn't going to look kindly on corporations that pay no taxes into the community chest. And those companies that refuse to pay a living wage? Well, she's not going to have a cozy fire for them.

Hestia Is a Goddess for Asexual and Aromantic People

In "Hymn V: To Aphrodite," "the pure maiden Hestia" is said to not "love Aphrodite's works."[8] Not only does she never marry, but there are no myths that attribute to her any lovers. That's pretty compelling evidence for seeing Hestia as a patron deity of asexual and aromantic people. If you are ace or aro or both, Hestia is your gal.

Creating a Partnership with Hestia

It might seem a contradiction that such a highly regarded goddess would have so few myths. She is rarely depicted in art. There are no Greek statues of Hestia. Those statues that survive are of Roman origin and often are of Vesta, the Roman goddess who was

---

8. *Hesiod, the Homeric Hymns, and Homerica*, "V: To Aphrodite," lines 17–18.

equivalated with Hestia. What vase paintings of Hestia there are often depict the goddess in a group setting. Those few portrayals show a young or middle-aged woman wearing a veil.

Hestia's Symbols, Herbs, and Crystals

For Greeks, Hestia was synonymous with the hearth she oversaw. Most altars to her bore no image or symbols associated with her, just the flame. She doesn't even have many symbols associated with her. The hog is sometimes associated with her due to it often being a sacrifice. The donkey, thanks to its waking her to Priapus's assault, is often linked to Hestia. Beyond that, however, there aren't any historical or mythological associations that have been passed down. With Hestia's name literally meaning "hearth" in Greek, the only symbol we can be sure of is the flame.

On the one hand this can be frustrating, especially to Pagans and witches who are used to deities coming with veritable tables full of plants, minerals, animals, and elements printed in books and on websites to use in setting up an altar space. This can also be a freeing experience, allowing those same people the chance to connect directly with Hestia. And there is a beauty in simplicity, really.

Hestia's Altar

The goddess Hestia, being one who didn't figure in major iconography and complicated worship, doesn't require an extensive altar. For most of my years working with her, I haven't gotten fancier than a candle. It is the placement of that candle that has been more meaningful. I've always placed it in my kitchen space. The candleholder is one my daughter made me in preschool. In that little bit of Mod Podge, crepe paper, and a baby food jar all the meaning of Hestia's devotion to the home lives.

Even when I wasn't actively working with Hestia, I had a small ritual when lighting the tea lights in that candleholder. As I struck the match, I would proclaim, "Hail, Hestia!" That ordinary action and those two words became the basis of our relationship and maintained our connection through those times when I felt most isolated.

At some point a small ceramic dish meant for holding sauces took up space before the candle. This is where I will pour a bit of oil or place a bit of the meal I've cooked as an offering to Hestia. This is an act of gratitude and acknowledgment of our relationship.

Next to the candle I keep the mortar and pestle. This is not as any part of an altar plan. It's just because I need a place to keep it, but I won't deny that over the years I've come to see it as part of my "Hestia space." Currently, a small golden pothos plant also occupies Hestia space, but that's more due to it just being convenient than anything else.

Hestia is not impressed by ornate altars. That's not to say you can't deck one out with crystals and goblets and the like, just that it's not necessary. She's a low-key goddess more interested in intent, focus, and action than fancy altar cloths and incense holders. So we're going to start simple and small: with the flame.

Find a candleholder that speaks of home to you, one that feels good when you hold it. One that looks good when your glance falls on it. You want something that *feels* good. This doesn't have to be the only candleholder either. If you like to change them out with the seasons or months or what have you, that's okay. The important thing is that whatever you choose, you feel a sense of *home* when you interact with it.

Next: candles. I use regular four-hour tea lights. This is because (1) that's what fits my holder, and (2) I can buy them in bulk and cheaply. You will have to decide what kind of candle you want to use.

Consider safety. Can you leave the candle burning when you aren't in the room, or will it be a danger to overhanging plants, cabinets, and so on? Will household pets or children get into it, causing harm? Will it set off smoke detectors? What is your budget? Do you have the means and attention to snuff a flame when needed? Obviously, you will not want to leave candles completely unattended, so if you opt for a flame that can last for hours, you have to be aware of extinguishing it if you leave your home.

Place your altar in the heart of your home. In this case it is the place you spend the most time. For me, it is the kitchen counter only because the kitchen is connected to the dining room, living room and hallway that leads to all other parts of the house. I pass my altar a dozen or more times a day, as does my family. This not only makes it the heart of my home but the area of the most traffic. The heart of your home could be the dresser in your bedroom or the entertainment center or the vanity in the bathroom. Only you can decide where that is. Hestia isn't going to judge where you place the altar.

You can add items to your altar like fresh-cut flowers, crystals and statues, and anything that helps foster your connection to Hestia. Spending some time in meditation or using a divination tool to speak to the goddess can help you better understand what should go with your altar.

 ### EXERCISE
Ritual for Connecting to Hestia

What you need:

> A candle in a candleholder
>
> Matches
>
> Paper and a writing utensil (optional)

Perform this ritual at a time when you won't be disturbed.

Set the candle in the holder on a table. Sit comfortably where you can easily reach the candle. Center and ground yourself (see section "Four Magickal Techniques" starting on page 27 for information on how to do this if you don't know how).

Light the candle. As you strike the match, say either aloud or in your mind, "Hail, Hestia!"

Cup your hands around the candleholder so that you can feel the heat against your skin.

Gaze at the flame and let your gaze go unfocused. Breathe evenly for a moment or two until you feel calm and present.

Say either aloud or in your mind, "Hestia, both first and last, come now to me that your presence and your influence might have a place in my life and my home." Be sincere when you do so. You are inviting Hestia to connect with you, even if only for a short time.

Wait for Hestia to come to you. Take note of any sensations that come to you. Do you smell anything or feel a presence? You may see something in the flame or the heat from the candle might take on a different intensity.

When you feel Hestia's presence, introduce yourself to her. Let her know why you are seeking to connect to her. Be as clear, honest, and concise as possible. Hestia isn't a deity who likes games or ambiguity.

Once you've said your piece, pay attention to anything she might relay to you.

Once you are finished, thank Hestia for her presence and any messages she gave you. Extinguish the candle.[9]

You can write down your observations from the ritual if you wish. This can be helpful, especially at the beginning of your work with Hestia, giving you details that will inform and shape how you approach her.

After making any notes, put away your things and have a drink of water or a bite to eat. Stretch or do an activity that gets you moving. This serves to not only get your circulation going but to bring you back to your body, as connecting with deities and spirits can sometimes leave you feeling a bit disjointed or "spacey." This is because interacting with such beings happens on nonphysical planes.

---

9. Usually, you will leave any candle you light for Hestia to burn out. Here, though, extinguishing the candle brings the ritual to a close.

How to Talk to Hestia

Hestia has been called by several epithets in the few mentions of her. She's been addressed as "pure maiden Hestia," "queenly maid," "fair goddess," "chief of the goddesses," "first of the gods," and even, in the "Hymn XXIV: To Hestia," she is described as having "soft oil dripping ever from [her] locks."[10] All of these are very formal.

In my experience Hestia wants to have a personal relationship. She's the aunt or uncle you turn to for advice, the grandmother who bakes your favorite treat, the sibling you share secrets with, and the friend who checks in on you. Hestia isn't out in the world somewhere but right at home.

When you first approach Hestia, treat it like you would contacting someone you want as a mentor. As the relationship progresses, you'll find that ceremony quickly falls to the wayside. I spend a good deal of my interactions with Hestia just talking to her as if with a friend. Even so, I will on occasion address her by title when I am invoking her to watch over my home and family.

Making Offerings

As the center of domestic life and the protector/progenitor of state religious life, Hestia was allocated the first portions of meals to honor her and show respect for and gratitude toward her. Traditionally, she was given offerings of bread and grains, cooking oil, salt, milk, wine, cider, rosemary, and thyme.

---

10. *Hesiod, the Homeric Hymns, and Homerica,* "V: To Aphrodite," lines 17, 23, and 32; Pindar, *Nemean Odes,* ode 11, lines 6–10, http://www.perseus.tufts.edu/hopper/text?doc=Perseus%3Atext%3A1999.01.0162%3Abook%3DN.%3Apoem%3D11; *Hesiod, the Homeric Hymns, and Homerica,* "XXIV: To Hestia," line 3.

When you start working with Hestia, make it a habit to give her daily offerings. These don't have to be elaborate or fancy. I have on occasion just placed some uncooked rice or oats in her offering dish as I am getting ready to cook. Other times I've added sprinkling of herbs or poured in some olive oil. To avoid issues with insects or pets getting into the offering, dispose of it before you retire to bed. You can place the offerings into a compost pile or the garbage.

When drinking, consider pouring out a libation to Hestia. If you are outside, pour a bit of your drink out onto the ground. Inside, pour a bit into the offering bowl. In either case, the important part is that you pour out the libation before you partake of it. Hestia is the first and the last. Part of showing gratitude is to offer up what we are giving thanks for to the deities first.

On occasion, you might want to perform a more involved offering. During ritual feasts, set a place for Hestia at your table. Keep a plate on your table, in the middle or off to the side where it won't be in the way. Add a small portion of everything you will be eating to the place before you sit down to eat. You can accompany this by giving thanks to Hestia aloud for those blessings you see in your life. Afterward, dispose of the food as you would other offerings. This can be a good activity to perform as a family, to introduce children and those interested in Paganism to various practices that go into Hestia's worship.

2
THE HOME:
AN ANATOMY OF COMFORT

The Scent of Lemon & Rosemary focuses on five key rooms of the house: the threshold, living room, kitchen, bathroom, and bedroom. The goal is to create a harmonious environment that fosters feelings of acceptance, safety, and abundance. In essence, you are going to balance the whole by addressing the individual energies of specific rooms. This goes beyond having one altar in one place in the house and turns the entire home into sacred space. You can use the crafts, spells, and rituals that follow whether you are the only person in your home or one of many. And if you are someone who doesn't have sole domain over the way the house is set up (if you are living with your parents, for example, or are not open about your magickal self with your roommates), many of those same rituals, spells, and crafts can be done without attracting any unwanted attention.

With the exception of the threshold, each section of the house has been associated with an element. The living room is the domain of the element of air, and we'll focus on energies of communication and ideas there. The kitchen is the domain of the element of fire and where we will be working with energies of love and peace. The bedroom is the domain of the element of earth and where we will work with energies of security and prosperity. And the bathroom is the domain of the element of water, and we'll focus on energies of purification and health.

The elements, and to a lesser extent the directions, play a major role in my practice. As the goddess of the hearth, Hestia is seen as a fire deity. But as pointed out in chapter 1, the hearth is more than just the fire that is set in the fireplace—it involves the entire home and the wider society. Life, the universe, and everything cannot be approached and experienced through a single element. And so, while this section assigns each room of the house to a certain element, this is not to be taken to mean only that element is to be found there. Houseplants, representatives of and belonging to the domain of earth, are often found in the living room. We light candles in the bathroom, associated with water, when we want to pamper ourselves in a bath. Water runs through the taps in the kitchen. The point is not to be inflexible with these assignments but to use them to organize the house in a way that makes sense and as a base from which to expand. Burn incense in your bedroom. Use crystals in your living room. Adapt what you learn in this book to your own unique needs.

Houses come in all shapes and sizes, from the one-room cabin nestled in the woods to the expansive mega-mansion that dominates the landscape. Most of us live in between those two extremes. The rooms covered in this book are found in most houses and apartments. However, if you live in a studio or a house with multiple living spaces, there are a few ways you can adapt this guidance to your own situation.

When I first moved to the Chicago area more than twenty years ago, I lived in a 600-foot studio. There was an enclosed bathroom. The kitchenette was open to the rest of the room. My bed was a sleeper sofa. In that case the space became a "bedroom" when I would unfold the couch at night. When it was put away during the day, I switched the way I viewed that space to include welcoming visitors. Such a rearranging of furniture is a way to compartmentalize your space.

You can also use physical objects to carve up the area of your studio. Assign bedroom status to your bed and living room status to the part of the studio where the couch and television sit. Use area rugs in the same way to create boundaries. Or you can use folding screens, curtains, or bookshelves to divide the space.

If none of those is an option, you can use visualization. Think about the space in the way that you are going to use it. For example, if friends are coming over, you would engage in your studio as if it were the living room. When you are alone and resting, you can then switch to treating it as a bedroom. This method does require you to be centered and comfortable with your space and have good visualization techniques. If you don't have experience with those concepts, I cover them in "Four Magickal Techniques" on page 27.

Currently, I live in a house with my husband and two children, two housemates, three cats, and a snake. Our home has to accommodate various lifestyles, work schedules, and personalities, which means the house is larger, and has more rooms, than my previous residence. For example, we have a living room and a finished basement, both of which serve similar functions: socializing and entertainment. If you are in a similar situation and find yourself spoiled for choice when it comes to having multiple rooms with overlapping functions, you have a couple of options on how to proceed.

The More the Merrier Method: Group rooms together by function. For example, in my home I would treat both the living room and the finished basement as the "living room." Any spells or rituals can be performed in both. This can be convenient when the kids are using the basement for games and I need to work my magick. This is a good strategy if multiple rooms are often used for the same function at the same time. We often will entertain people in both the living room and the basement during holidays. I can work spells for cooperation in either of the rooms, but I work in both to make them spaces of comfort and relaxation for everyone.

The There Can Be Only One Method: Choose one of the rooms as the space where you will perform your living room rituals and spells. If our basement served only as the overflow space for when we had guests over, then I would focus on the living room. Likewise, when you consider your house, you might realize that when people are over, you spend more time in the family room than the formal living room. Maybe you find that your family tends to congregate in the dining room when they are all home. What matters is that you choose a place that is meant to be a public part of the home (as opposed to a bed-room).

Whatever your house situation, whatever way you delineate your space, it is important to be consistent after you have decided. The more you practice in a designated space, the easier it becomes. The space gets "seasoned" as you raise the energies related to the room. Eventually, your home will become so steeped in energies of creativity, prosperity, love, and well-being that people who have never set foot in your home will feel it the moment they enter.

Read through the later sections on the threshold, kitchen, liv-ing room, bedroom, and bathroom with your own home in mind. Designate one room or a section to each of these five areas. When you have decided, go to each room, or space, and tell Hestia, "This is (fill in the blank)" either aloud or in your mind. This way you are both introduced to the space and its function, and you both start out on the same page. Include your family in this exercise if they are also part of your practice.

3

MAKING MAGICK

This chapter covers several subjects that need to be addressed now, as they'll be used throughout the rest of the book. If you aren't new to witchcraft, some of the concepts covered in the "Four Magickal Techniques" and "Charms" sections are going to be old hat for you. If this is your first foray into spellwork or you feel like you need a refresher, you'll want to read those sections to understand what is required of you later in the book.

The "Materia Magica" section covers the items you will be using regularly in the spells and rituals throughout the book. It goes into detail on how the items will be used, their magickal properties, and any substitutions, if applicable. The last two sections involve techniques for making some essential materials and tools needed for both spellwork and rituals in this book.

Four Magickal Techniques

There are four techniques you'll encounter throughout the book that deal with one's state of mind and magick (or will): visualization, centering, grounding, and raising power. Various different magick practitioners view and define the way spells are created, fueled, and cast in different ways. Magick is a personal matter and everyone experiences it in a way that is particular to them. There are general similarities, of course. It is like the matter of language and thoughts. If I am with a group of people and say the word *cat*, each person will call to mind a different image of a cat. There might even be some who don't visualize a cat but hear one purring or feel soft fur. All the people in the group, however, recognize the word and understand that I mean the small domesticated feline.

It is the same with much of magick. When I am working a spell, I envision that I am manipulating energies to manifest my will. I experience energy from myself as a physical sensation. You may have a different experience. If you've never worked magick before, you might even wonder if you are doing it right. This is when the four practices that follow will be useful. They will help you figure out what magick feels like to you. They are four tools that can help beyond spellcasting.

Visualization

If you've done any magick, you'll have been introduced to the concept of visualization. It is the grown-up word for imagination, which is unfortunate because I think imagination is a better description for what you are doing. However, imagination carries with it the connotation of make-believe and invention, which can undercut the power of magick. For the sake of consistency with established norms, we'll use the term *visualization*. I want to point out that visualization isn't limited to just images. Visualization can include scents, tastes, sounds, and sensations. Not everyone is visually inclined, and if you have trouble "seeing" things in your mind, explore other senses.

Visualization, in all its forms, is key to magick. Magick often requires you to interact with planes beyond the physical. It requires, essentially, for you to be able to tap into your imagination to make it work. You'll come across exercises later that will ask you to visualize certain things. To get you in practice, and to get you familiar with Hestia, go through the exercise that follows.

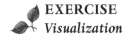

EXERCISE
Visualization

Sit comfortably and think about Hestia. Based on everything you read in chapter 1, what do you imagine she looks like? What color is her hair? Is it long? Short? How does she dress? What is her skin tone? Is she tall? Short? If it helps, close your eyes, so you can focus on building an image in your mind of what Hestia looks like to you. The fact that she has not been represented often in Greek art means that you have the freedom to imagine her however you want.

Now think about how she sounds. Is her voice low or soft or loud? Does she speak with an accent? What kind of language does she use? Does she use slang? Does she sound like someone you know, or is the voice you hear completely new to you?

How does she smell? How does she walk? Are her hands smooth or rough? What is she doing as you visualize her?

You may not visualize her in a human form at all. Maybe she is a dancing flame or a hot wind. The point of the exercise is to practice visualization and to investigate how Hestia appears when you start working with her.

Write down what you came up with. Later, once you've been working with Hestia for a while, return to those notes and see if your impressions have changed in any way.

Centering

Ever feel overwhelmed, pulled in a dozen different directions, or unable to concentrate? If you can't focus, you can't work magick.

Centering, simply, is bringing your awareness to your body. You are pulling your focus inward and blocking any outside thoughts and sensations, if only for a few seconds. There is a plethora of meditation techniques that have centering as their goal, and I encourage you to research and try out many to find one that works for you. For the purposes of this book, however, I'm going to provide a short, quick exercise to practice several times a day.

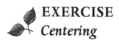

EXERCISE
Centering

To start, become aware of your body. If you are sitting, settle your feet on the floor, rest your hands on your thighs, straighten your spine, and lengthen your neck. If you are standing, set your feet hip width apart and let your hands and arms fall to your sides. Straighten your spine and lengthen your neck. Close your eyes. Take a deep breath in. It should be deep enough that you fill your lungs and expand your diaphragm and long enough to be comfortable. Hold the breath for a few seconds and then exhale completely. Draw in another deep breath. Do not strain. Now let your consciousness sink into your body. Check in with your feet and legs, hands and arms, belly, chest, shoulder, neck, and head. You are just acknowledging your body, being in it; do not judge your body, but accept it as it is. Once you've done this, let your attention focus on your belly, heart, or whatever area that you feel is your center.

Visualize all of your non-physical body contracting and pulling into that center. Your aura or psychic body, any energies that might extend beyond your skin, and even any emotions that might be especially pronounced at the moment can be reeled in. Visualize your consciousness sinking into your center. Rest for a moment in this place. You should be breathing deeply throughout this exercise. Once you feel settled into your center, breathe out a long breath and open your eyes. You can roll your shoulders, stretch, or wiggle your toes and fingers. The whole exercise should take no more than thirty seconds, but it can take some time and practice to get to that point. Practice this exercise for a week to start. As you gain confidence and proficiency with this new skill, you'll find you can do it no matter where you are at or what is going on around you. Before any ritual or spellwork, you will center yourself.

Grounding

Grounding is the opposite of centering. Instead of drawing your attention inward, you are sending it outward. Specifically, you are sending any disruptive energies or feelings out of your body by sending them into the earth. Grounding can be used alone or in conjunction with centering. The earth is the great transformer. Everything including fallen leaves, dead plants, spoor, bodies, and so on is taken into the earth and turned into the soil, which nurtures new growth. It is this cycle that is behind the concept of grounding. Using your visualization, you push negative emotions or energies into the earth, where they are transformed into something more beneficial. It is a type of unburdening. As with centering, grounding is an exercise you should practice often.

EXERCISE
Grounding

You can do this exercise either sitting or standing. As you sit or stand, start deep breathing. You want to fill your lungs and expand your belly, but without strain. Hold the breath for three to seven seconds and then exhale fully. Visualize roots emerging from the soles of your feet (if standing) or from the bottom of your spine (if sitting). The roots enter the earth, connecting you to the rich, black soil. Visualize any negative emotions, thoughts, or energies draining out of you through those roots into the earth. As soon as they touch the soil, these burdensome energies get absorbed and transmuted into nutrients that can stimulate future growth. Once all that you wish to unburden has drained out of you, visualize your roots withdrawing back into your body. Give thanks to the earth for taking it all in.

As with centering, you should ground before every ritual or spellcraft.

Raising Power

This is where the magickal rubber hits the magickal road. Spell and magick working involves manipulating energy. Want a new job? In addition to sending out resumes, updating your social networks, and filling out applications, you might want to give your job search a magickal boost. To this end, you might work a spell to attract the perfect job or a spell to make you appear as the perfect candidate at an interview. Boiled down to basics, this is just attempting to assert your own will onto the workings of the universe. And all of that works like driving a car. The car is the spell. The destination is the goal of the spell. You are the driver, maneuvering the car to that destination. What powers the car is the energy you harness and pour into it. That energy can come from various sources. Of course obstacles can arise along the way: there can be traffic, roads can be under construction, there might be tolls, and so on. But you can make decisions and take actions that can perhaps avoid or overcome those difficulties.

So raising energy is like putting gas in the car. You can add your own energy to spells or draw from other sources, such as materia magica, by tapping into the timing of spells, or having spirit helpers, deities, and so on aid you. What you are going to do is take in the energies from different sources, funnel them all together, and then send that energy into the spell.

Raising energy comes after you've centered and grounded yourself. This ensures that you won't have any errant, detrimental energies getting into the mix. If you are fueling a spell from your own personal magick energy, you need only draw upon it and then send it, either into an object if you are making a talisman or charm or out into the universe if it is a spell. It might take practice to get the visualization right. Use the exercise below to hone your skills at perceiving the magickal energies of various materia magica.

EXERCISE
Sensing Magickal Energy

It took me years to understand what magick felt like to me. Part of that was due to the haphazardness of my practice. It wasn't until I made a practice of centering and grounding before working a spell that I became aware of the sensations around and in me when I worked magick. For me, raising my energy for a spell is a physical sensation akin to a tingling that originates between my shoulder blades. With continued effort, I got to the point where I could move that sensation down my arms to my hands and then out into whatever spell I was working on. With more practice I was able to recognize similar sensations in various materials. Sometimes I experienced these energies as sensations, or as smells, colors, sounds, and the like. As you do the exercise, you'll have your own experience.

For this exercise, you will need:

> Candle
>
> Piece of paper
>
> Writing utensil
>
> Fan of some sort
>
> Small container of soil or salt
>
> Small container of water

Sit comfortably with the items lined up before you. Center and ground yourself. Light the candle and observe it. Let your gaze soften as you watch the flame. What sensation does it generate in you? Don't try to filter or censor your responses. Spend a minute on the candle, then jot down any scents, images, or feelings that came to you. Once you've written down everything that came to you, turn your focus to the fan. Turn it on and repeat the observation and documentation steps. Work your way through the soil or salt and the water. Once you are done, read over your notes. Now is the time for analysis. These are clues to how you experience the energies of the various elements.

You can repeat this exercise with various items, such as crystals, herbs, and flowers. Doing so allows you to build a personal dictionary of magickal energies.

 **EXERCISE**
Hestia's Energy

Light a candle and invite Hestia to join you. Observe the candle while bringing Hestia to mind. Write down whatever sensations come to mind. Repeat this exercise two more times. Compare these sensations to what you feel when you are making offerings to Hestia, lighting the candle at her altar, and so on. How does Hestia's energy feel to you? What does it smell, taste, look, and sound like?

Extra credit: once you've established Hestia's energy, practice calling up that energy when you aren't engaged in communion or magick workings. Try doing so in the least Pagan or witchy setting, like riding public transport or waiting in line at the bank. Congratulations, you have established a way to invoke Hestia without elaborate rituals, invocations, or materials.

Charms

When you charm an item, you are using your own energy to program it with a particular magickal intent. The concept is similar to making a talisman; however, you are using everyday items to accomplish magickal goals. Typically, those goals are smaller and more specific than the jobs talismans are tasked with. Instead of protecting a home, such as with the Protective Door Talisman on page 61, you might charm your keychain so that your keys are never lost.

To charm items, hold them in your hands or hold your dominant hand over them, and pour a little of your personal magickal energy into them. Envision the energy like a light that cascades into the item and then sinks into it. As you do so, also pour your intention into the energy.

For example, if you are charming your chapstick so that your words are persuasive, hold the chapstick, and as you energize it, say, "My words are heeded" or perhaps "My advice is followed." Afterward, whenever you apply the chapstick, your speech will have a magickal boost.

Materia Magica

Throughout *The Scent of Lemon & Rosemary*, you'll find many items are used often in various recipes and spells. These materia magica have been chosen for not only their magickal properties, but for their multiple uses, versatility, and availability. Everything, with the exception of the beeswax and perhaps the essential oils, can be gotten at any local grocery store. Stocking up on the materials shouldn't cost you too much, and their commonplace uses shouldn't raise any questions if you are practicing in secret. Once you've read through the descriptions, I recommend going through your pantry to see what you already have on hand and then filling it out with the rest. While I am all for flexibility and encourage you to substitute any other item in the later spells and recipes, the items in this section really can't be substituted.

Fortunately, with regard to the essential oils, arguably the most expensive materia magica, a little goes a long way and a small bottle will last you a long time.

Routine spell ingredients are as follows:

- Olive oil
- Lemons
- Rosemary
- Thyme
- Salt
- Witch hazel or vodka
- Vinegar
- Baking soda
- Beeswax (or soy or candelilla wax)
- Various essential oils
- Water

Olive Oil

The olive tree, and thus olives and olive oil by extension, has had deeply significant religious and magickal properties over millennia. According to Greek mythology, the first olive tree sprung up in a city in Attica. The city was newly formed and in need of a patron god. Both Athena and Poseidon desired to fill that need and claim the city as their own. To settle the matter, a contest was arranged, organized either by Zeus or the city's king, depending on the source of the myth. Both gods were to present gifts to the city. The one who provided the best gift would then be awarded guardianship. In some tellings, Poseidon struck a stone in the center of the city and a saltwater well sprung up. In others, his creation of the first horses was his gift. All versions agree that when it came time to present her gift, Athena drove her spear into the ground and the first olive tree sprouted. Athena won the contest and the city was named Athens, with the olive tree becoming sacred to her.

Olive trees were cultivated as early at 6000 BCE throughout Asia Minor, making olive oil the first vegetable oil used by people in the area.[11] It was used for cooking, lighting lamps, making cosmetics and soap, and religious and ritual purposes. No wonder it has been so important to the Mediterranean from antiquity to modern times. This connection with Greek mythology is one reason olive oil features so prominently in my work with Hestia. There are centuries of layered and established association between the oil and Greek gods, which you can tap into to enhance your workings.

Olive oil is also readily available and economical. And its versatility means you can use it for ritual, magickal, religious, and culinary purposes. Olive oil is associated with the sun and has magickal properties of healing, peace, and protection. In the culinary recipes later in the book, olive oil is used to create a connection with the Divine, either Hestia or another deity you are working with. Keep a bottle of extra-virgin olive oil on hand for the various spells, rituals, and recipes throughout the book.

Lemon

Lemons have been suggested as being the "golden apples" from Hera's garden, which were guarded by the Hesperides. A hybrid between a bitter orange and a citron, the lemon's origin is unknown, though regions of India and China have been suggested

---

11. Alice Alech and Cécile Le Galliard, *The 7 Wonders of Olive Oil* (New York: Familius, 2017), 11.

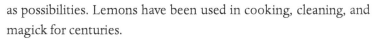

as possibilities. Lemons have been used in cooking, cleaning, and magick for centuries.

Magickally, lemons have properties of purification, love, and blessings. They are associated with the moon and can be used in any spells that could benefit from the presence of moon energies. They are used as an enhancer to magick, so add some lemon to your spells to give them a magickal boost. Because of their purification powers, lemons are especially useful in cleansing sprays and incenses. Symbolically, lemons represent joy, happiness, and fulfillment, which you can tap into by keeping a number of lemons in a bowl on your kitchen counter.

In cooking, lemons are a flavor enhancer and preserver, as the ascorbic acid in them helps stop browning due to oxidation in cut fruits and vegetables. They also help steamed vegetables maintain their bright colors. They are high in vitamin C and other nutrients.

In cleaning, lemons act as an odor remover and can lighten stains. The acid in them is antibacterial and antiseptic. The oil in the peel breaks down grease. The peels can be soaked in distilled white vinegar for two weeks to create a base for cleaning solutions with a pleasant aroma.

Rosemary

Rosemary is native to the Mediterranean. Its name derives from Latin and means "dew of the sea." In Greek mythology rosemary was said to have draped Aphrodite when she emerged from the sea.

It is a perennial plant that can be trimmed into various shapes. One winter solstice I bought a potted rosemary plant that had been shaped into a form of an evergreen tree. The whole season my home was filled with the most wonderful scent. Unfortunately, I didn't have the knowledge to keep the plant alive.

If you decide to grow rosemary, know that the roots cannot stand to be wet, so if you have a potted plant, make sure it has excellent drainage. Rosemary is difficult to start from seed, so you might be better off buying an already established plant. Rosemary that is grown out of doors will need some extra care if the winter months are especially cold to ensure it survives to spring.

Rosemary has magickal properties of protection, love, mental powers, purification, healing, and sleep. It is associated with the sun and with the element of fire. It is associated with the goddess Aphrodite. According to Cunningham, rosemary, when burnt, rids a space of negativity, "especially prior to performing magic."[12] Bundles of dried rosemary can be burnt to purify an area.

Culinarily, rosemary is used in a variety of dishes. Sprigs can be added to soups and stews, while the dried herb can be used in casseroles, in pilafs, and with potatoes and other vegetables.

Rosemary essential oil can be added to cleaning products, especially sprays or floor washes, to add a pleasant scent.

Thyme

Thyme is the only other herb that is used extensively throughout the book. It is another plant native to the Mediterranean. The common and Latin name (*Thymus*) comes from the Greek word *thumus*, which means courage. It is another evergreen perennial that is slightly easier to grow than rosemary. I have on several occasions kept potted thyme in my garden, giving it the barest of attention, and it just grows on, offering up fragrant sprigs for soups, stuffings, and incense. Thyme can also be grown indoors as part of a windowsill herb garden. Thyme is more than a culinary herb,

12. Scott Cunningham, *Cunningham's Encyclopedia of Magical Herbs* (St. Paul, MN: Llewellyn Publications, 1985), 219.

however. Thyme is often used in teas to soothe sore throats (when a tea of it is gargled) and for coughs (when used in a steam).

Thyme is associated with the element of water. It has magickal properties of healing, sleep, psychic powers, love, purification, and courage. This is the herb you want to slip into any talismans to aid you in conflict. Under a pillow it "ensures restful sleep and a pleasant lack of nightmares" and is burned before "magical rituals to cleanse the area," Cunningham writes. Taking a magical cleansing bath of thyme and marjoram in the spring will cleanse one of past ills and sorrows.[13]

It's thyme's magickal and medicinal properties that put it on the list of required materia magica; however, its culinary uses shouldn't be overlooked. As with rosemary, sprigs of the herb can be added to soups and stews, while the dried herb, along with minced garlic and lemon juice, give flavor to rice and pasta dishes.

Salt

The word *salary* is derived from the word *salt*, a testament to how the mineral was one of the first measures of commerce and wealth. One of the earliest known towns established in Europe was a salt mining town in Bulgaria, founded around 4000 BCE. Salt's importance isn't surprising. As one of the first preservatives, it was essential to putting up the bounty of the harvest for use during lean times.

Magickally, salt has properties of protection and purification. It can absorb energies, a useful trait for cleansing areas. It is associated with the earth, even those forms that come from the ocean. Ritually, salt can be used as an offering.

---

13. Cunningham, *Cunningham's Encyclopedia of Magical Herbs*, 209.

There are several types of salt to be had, including sea salt, kosher salt, Epsom salt, pink Himalayan salt, table salt, and fancy finishing/culinary salts. For the purposes of the spells, recipes, and rituals in this book, sea salt is all you need. I don't recommend using table salt in spells, as the iodine and anticaking agents that are added to it can change or even interfere with the magickal properties. Some culinary salts will have added ingredients, such as herbs (think garlic salt) that will bring their own magickal qualities to the mix, so make sure that you know exactly what is in your salt before you use it.

In spellwork there is a mixture called black salt that is used for protective magick. Black salt is simply salt mixed with ashes so that it has a black color. Some might add black food coloring or dye to the mixture to make the color more intense, but that can result in a messy mixture that needs to be dried out before it can be used. Another way to make your own black salt is through burning loose incense.

Charcoal discs can burn up to 1,500 degrees Fahrenheit, meaning you will need a fireproof dish. I use a small cast-iron cauldron, which I set on a trivet to protect the surface I'm using. A stone bowl or another container specifically meant for incense should work. Glass isn't recommended, as the high temperature can shatter it. Be sure you are using charcoal discs that are meant for burning incense. Your ordinary barbeque briquette is going to give off fumes you shouldn't be inhaling.

In your dish, pour two tablespoons of sea salt. On top of the salt place a charcoal disc used to burn incense. You can either light the disc and burn it on its own or add dried herbs (such as rosemary or thyme) to add their protective properties to the mix. Let the disc burn completely and then cool. Pour the salt and ashes into a mortar and pestle and mix, grinding down any chunks of the ash and incorporating the ash and salt evenly. Keep the resultant black salt in a tightly sealed container when not in use.

Witch Hazel

Witch hazel (*Hamamelis virginiana*) is a small shrub or tree that is native to the Americas. The common name comes from an Old English word that means "pliant and to bend," but that doesn't mean we can't enjoy the modern connotation of a plant with witch in the name.[14] You can find witch hazel in various stores as an extract. The extract is made from the leaves and branches and is then distilled with alcohol or water. For years it was used in beauty and medicinal recipes.

Magickally, witch hazel is associated with the sun and the element of fire. It has properties of banishing, hex-breaking, and protection, making it a good additive to room sprays for areas that have been the target of magick or psychic attacks. If someone is coming into your house after being somewhere magickally negative, you can spray them with a mixture of water and witch hazel to help cleanse them of any lingering harmful energies. Alternatively, you can hang branches of witch hazel over your door to protect your home. Witch hazel also helps amplify the magickal energies of essential oils and magickal sprays in that it can anchor or "fix" those energies to an area.

Witch hazel has antibacterial properties and reduces swelling and itching on skin, which is one of the reasons it has long been used as a facial toner. The extract helps mix essential oils and water and also helps scents linger. Throughout the book, witch hazel is used in beauty and spray recipes, as well as spells.

---

14. *Online Etymological Dictionary*, s.v. "witch hazel," accessed September 28, 2020, https://www.etymonline.com/word/witch%20hazel.

Vodka

While witch hazel is amazing in the variety of ways it can be used, it cannot be taken internally, which is where vodka comes in. In actuality, any alcohol can be used with the recipes throughout this book, and in fact there's something to be said for just a hot whiskey toddy to soothe a cold and help one sleep. However, I use vodka for several reasons. Vodka is tasteless. It can be made from a variety of plants (potatoes, sorghum, corn, wheat), which means that you can bring the properties of those plants into your spellwork.

Magickally, vodka is associated with the element of fire. It has properties of protection and purification. Add a few drops to your spells to protect them from being countered or turned from their goal. Asperge a space with vodka to purify it before performing spellwork. Pour out a shot of vodka when working outdoors as an offering to genius loci before performing spellwork or a ritual. Leave a shot on your altar for Hestia.

Vodka has antibacterial and antimildew properties, which make it useful in bathroom cleaning applications. Like witch hazel, it helps essential oils and water mix and evaporates without leaving a residue, so it can also be used in room sprays. Though the amount of alcohol in tinctures is minimal, vegetable glycerin can be substituted for vodka in tincture recipes.

Vinegar

Once upon a time, so the story goes, a plague descended upon the land and many people died. In the midst of this tragedy a group of four thieves were caught robbing the dead. When they were brought before the judge, they bargained for their freedom by offering to reveal how they had avoided catching the plague as they robbed graves. The judge agreed and they turned over a recipe of vinegar and other spices. That is the story of four thieves vinegar that has been used medicinally and magickally for years. There's no information on how the fabled vinegar was used, either internally or externally, but similar vinegar recipes, such as one written about by René-Maurice Gattefossé, instructed readers, "Use by rubbing it on the hands, ears and temples from time to time when approaching a plague victim."[15]

Magickally, vinegar is associated with the element of fire. It has protective properties, especially dealing with psychic protection. Its cleansing magickal properties are useful in baths, where its strong scent can be mitigated by other fragrant spell components. Use it in spells that require a length of time (more than a month) to work, as its preservative properties will give the spell the longevity it needs to accomplish its goal. Use it in spellwork meant to secure and preserve one's health. Vinegar can also be used in magick tinctures and infusions that are meant to be ingested.

Vinegar is used not only in cooking but also in preserving foods. Every summer I toss a portion of our cucumber haul from the garden into a bowl of vinegar, water, salt, and pepper for easy refrigerator pickles. I also keep a bottle of balsamic vinegar on hand to mix with olive oil for salad dressings. Since vinegar can be made by fermenting any ingredient that contains ethanol alcohol, there is a world of different vinegars available to use, each with differing characteristics and flavors depending on their source.

Vinegar has antibacterial properties and kills mold and germs. Common white vinegar has a 5-percent acidity, which is enough to break down most stains and mineral deposits without being harmful to people or pets. Because of this and the fact that it is widely

---

15. René-Maurice Gattefossé, *Gattefossé's Aromatherapy,* trans. C. W. Daniel Company (Essex, England: C. W. Daniel Company, 1993), 85–86.

available and economical, it is the backbone of most "green" cleaning products.

Baking Soda

Yes, baking soda is great for absorbing odors in the refrigerator. Yes, it is necessary for baking. But using baking soda in magick? Well, yes. Baking soda, also known as sodium bicarbonate, is a salt and alkaline in nature, which means when it comes in contact with an acid, like for instance vinegar or lemon juice, it will react in a vigorous fizzing. This reaction may be chemical, but that doesn't mean it isn't also magickal.

Magickally, baking soda is associated with the earth element. It has magickal properties of banishing and purification, but these powers are based on its absorptive abilities, so if you are using baking soda in any kind of cleansing magick, it will need to be discarded elsewhere; otherwise the energies it absorbed will linger. Baking soda also does not discriminate between good and negative energies. It is a good component to use when you need to completely "wipe" a space. If you want to do the same for yourself, soak in a bath with baking soda, drain all the water, and then bathe again with protective spell components or shower using an herb bundle or scrub to add a protective magickal layer.

Baking soda is a staple in making household cleaners because it is mildly abrasive and cuts through grease.

Beeswax

Beeswax is a material made by honeybees (in the genus *Apis*) that they build their combs from. Those combs are harvested along with the honey by beekeepers. The wax is then melted down and processed for use. While there is a very romantic notion of beeswax candles being used in previous centuries, they were expensive and most people depended on rushes or candles made from animal tallow. Today, beeswax is more widely available. A quick search on the internet should turn up local apiaries where you can purchase it. Beeswax is used in candles, salves, talismans, and more.

Magickally, beeswax is associated with both Aphrodite and Hephaestus, which, when taken into the context of the mythology and modern representations of that Olympian couple, could be viewed as ironic. When you need a spell to work without a hitch, when you are trying to deal with mechanical or industrial issues, or when you are interested in creating something that is both beautiful and functional, add beeswax to your spellwork. It also works as a binding agent, getting the various spell components to work together in harmony. Beeswax also has magickal properties of prosperity, community, wisdom, and messages. If you are trying to get a group of people to work together on a common goal, write the goal on a piece of paper, fold it, and seal it with beeswax. Carry the resulting talisman with you to any meetings for the project.

Beeswax has antioxidant and anti-inflammatory properties, which is why it is often included in beauty products and salves. It also has a lush and rich aroma that just makes the products you use feel extra luxurious.

You can substitute candelilla, soy, or bayberry wax for beeswax in the recipes throughout this book. However, make sure you research those ingredients for their specific magickal properties to see how they will react to your spellwork, and you may have to adjust the quantities in the recipes to get the best results.

Essential Oils

The last item in this section is the one most open to adjustment and personal preferences. Essential oils are compounds that have been extracted from plants. As their name suggests, they are oils, but not in the sense of, say, olive oil. They are concentrated and should not be ingested or placed directly onto the skin. Essential oils need to be diluted in a carrier oil or in a recipe.

Make sure the oils you buy are 100 percent pure. Some companies will cut down essential oils with fillers or synthetic ingredients that not only dilute the various properties of the oil, but can leave you with something that smells like chemicals. Because it can take a great deal of plant material to produce only small amounts of oil, you might find some to be expensive. Fortunately, a little goes a long way, and most recipes are only going to call for ten to twenty drops of a certain oil.

To start off, you might want to pick up peppermint and lavender essential oils. You can expand your collection to tea tree, lemon eucalyptus, basil, orange, and other oils, depending on your needs. There are some companies that create essential oil blends for calming the mind, spiritual blessing, and more. As long as you are making sure that the blends use pure essential oils and no fillers, they can be useful additions to your apothecary. Store your oils in a cool place away from heat and light when you aren't using them.

How to Make Herb-Infused Oil

Infused oils give you access to the magical and medicinal properties of plants. They have a plethora of applications—from anointing to kitchen witchery. They give you plenty of opportunities to flex your creative muscles. Plus, they are fun to make in a stirring-the-cauldron, making-a-magick-potion way.

The oil you use is called the carrier oil. Extra-virgin olive oil is suitable for most applications. You can experiment with other oils too. Oils like almond, grapeseed, safflower, and avocado all give you plenty of options when it comes to matching the properties of oils to your purpose.

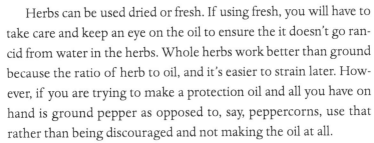
Herbs can be used dried or fresh. If using fresh, you will have to take care and keep an eye on the oil to ensure the it doesn't go rancid from water in the herbs. Whole herbs work better than ground because the ratio of herb to oil, and it's easier to strain later. However, if you are trying to make a protection oil and all you have on hand is ground pepper as opposed to, say, peppercorns, use that rather than being discouraged and not making the oil at all.

If you are making an oil that is not meant to be taken internally (for dressing candles versus using in baking, for example), you don't have to limit yourself to herbs when infusing the oil. You can add crystals or stones, metals, objects of power, and other materia magica to your jar along with your herbs. Taking the protection oil mentioned as an example above, you could add pins or a piece of glass to add a sharpness to your spell, a piece of jet for its protective properties, and a charm in the shape of a pentagram to enhance and strengthen the magick.

When adding any ingredient to your oil—herb, crystal, metal, or other—make sure that it won't add moisture to the oil, thus turning it rancid. Also, if using inorganic materials, check to see if the oil will harm them, especially if they are items you want to be able to use again. Finally, always keep your purpose in mind, and if the oil is meant to be consumed, make sure you aren't including anything that is poisonous.

As for tools, you'll need a saucepan, a jar with a lid, and cheesecloth or a sieve. The jar can be anything from a reused salsa container (cleaned thoroughly, of course) to a fancy bottle you bought specifically for this purpose. Use what is available to you and what makes you happy. Hestia is a low-key goddess who doesn't get caught up in appearances. The jar has to have a lid that seals tightly as you'll be shaking it. The jar should be large enough to hold all your ingredients and enough oil to cover everything with an inch of headspace (space between the top of the contents and the lid).

1. Fill a saucepan with 2 to 3 inches of water.

2. Add the herbs (and any other ingredients) to the jar.

3. Pour oil into the jar until it covers the herbs completely.

4. Place the jar in the saucepan. The water in the saucepan should sit several inches below the rim of the jar. You want to avoid any water getting into your oil.

5. Turn on the heat and bring the water to just below a boil. You don't want large bubbles that might spray water into your oil. Any water will introduce the opportunity for the oil to go rancid.

6. Once the water has just started to boil, turn the heat off. Let the water cool completely. Remove the jar and place the lid on it.

7. Set the jar aside for about 24 hours. If you are creating an oil with sun properties or that will be used in any spells or projects that would benefit from solar energy, place it in a sunny spot. If you need it to have moon properties, place it in a dark place, pulling it out at night and placing the jar where moonlight can fall on it. Wherever you place the jar, give it a shake every few hours.

8. Using the cheesecloth or a sieve, strain the herbs from the oil. You can use the oil immediately or bottle it for later. The oil can be stored in a cool, dry place for up to 6 months.

Hestia Anointing Oil

Anointing oils are used to mark people and objects. The purpose can be to prepare for ritual, to consecrate a tool for magickal work, or to invoke deities, spirits, or even elements. It can also be used in spellwork to dress candles.

Using the instructions for herb-infused oil starting on page 48, you'll be making an anointing oil specifically for working with Hestia. You'll be using the oil to do the following:

- Mark your altar, ritual tools, cauldron, or any other item you use in spellwork
- Anoint talismans or amulets for yourself, friends, and family to carry Hestia's protection
- Mark the outside of your front door to invoke Hestia's protection on your home
- Dress candles for any candle magick where you want Hestia's blessing
- Add it to your cooking to bring Hestia's energy of home, comfort, and family into the food you are making
- Use to anoint yourself before meditations or journeys where you wish to engage with Hestia

You'll need olive oil and rosemary leaves. You can use fresh or dried rosemary. Note that each results in oils that look and smell differently. Dried rosemary can often have a scent resembling pine. Magickally and medicinally, this doesn't make a difference, but if you will be using this oil in cooking, you might want to try both types and see which one you prefer. Before you add your herbs to the jar, crush them slightly, either with your hands or a mortar and pestle, to help release their natural oils.

Fill your jar about-a third full of the rosemary leaves. Then cover with the oil and follow the directions in the previous section.

Time the making of your oil to the full moon. If you celebrate a holiday that emphasizes family and prosperity, you could draw on that energy and make the oil. Even better if you can get your family involved. This is an easy project that even young children can help with, especially the shaking part at the end. That sense of togetherness will imbue the ingredients, which in turn will increase the potency of your resulting oil.

When you are shaking the jar, visualize Hestia's fire permeating the oil. Cup it in your hands a moment and feel the warmth transferring from your palms to the glass and then into the bottle. Feel that connection with Hestia and visualize the ways you will be making use of the oil once it is finished. Spend a bit of time completely in the moment of what you are doing.

Water Magick

Water is a common ingredient in magick. It is used for ritual cleansing, as a base for various tinctures and infusions, in kitchen witchery, and as a direct connection to the magickal, mystical, and spiritual properties of the element of water. Water is everywhere, but some types are better suited to magick than others. There are two types of water that are used throughout the book: moon water and distilled water.

Moon Water

If you've had any experience with Pagan or witchcraft practices, you might already be familiar with moon water. This is water that has been charged by the full moon, so it carries in it the powers and properties of the moon. These properties involve emotions, dreams, divination, secrets, shielding, and even pulling in the astrological energies of the sign the moon is passing through at the time. Even further refinement of the energies can be accomplished based on whether the moon is eclipsed, what the weather is like, the month of the year, and so on. This makes moon water extremely versatile.

To make moon water, fill a jar or bowl with water on the night of a full moon. Place your container of water out where moonlight will fall on it, charging the water inside. You can take this process a step further by silvering your water. This is a technique wherein you hold your container so that the moon is reflected in the water, thus "silvering" it.

You can then use the water immediately, or you can bottle it for later use. If you store your moon water, make sure to label the container with the date it was made. Add any other notes that you feel are relevant, such as the sign the moon was passing through, if the moon was full during a sabbat, even what moon it was (February's Pisces moon will have a distinctly different energy than September's Libra moon, for example).

If you make it a habit to make moon water each month, you could quickly end up with an apothecary full of various "flavors" of water to cover nearly all of your spellcasting needs. Some uses for moon water include adding it to the following:

- Your coffeemaker to infuse your morning coffee
- Household cleaners
- Salt dough or paste offerings
- Tinctures
- Spell jars

Distilled Water

Distilled water is useful for practical, rather than magickal, reasons. Distilled water is water that has been purified by being boiled into vapor and then collected. Many impurities are left behind in the boiling process, leaving a water that is less likely to clog things or leave behind deposits. It is especially useful for making room sprays, using in philters and infusions, and using in magick spells.

Distilled water can be bought, but you can also make your own at home. To make distilled water, you will need a large pot with a lid and a smaller pot or bowl that fits easily inside the larger one. Fill the large pot about halfway full with water and place it on a burner of a stove or hot plate. Place the smaller pot or bowl in this water, making sure that its sides rise higher than the water in the larger pan. Place the lid on the pot upside down. This will direct the water vapor to the center, where it will drip down to be collected in the bowl. Place ice or an ice pack on the lid. This will speed up the condensation process. Turn on the heat to medium high so that the water comes to a low boil. Let the water boil for about an hour, replacing the ice as it melts (you can use a turkey baster to remove the water). Be sure to use protection when changing the ice, as the lid and pot will be hot.

This process won't give you a lot of water quickly. An hour of work will net you about a cup of water. Most projects don't require a lot of distilled water, however. You can also spend a few hours making up a whole batch that you can then store for later use. Make sure you label the water when you store it.

4

THE THRESHOLD:
PROTECTING YOUR HOME

The entrance to a house is a necessary vulnerability. We must have a way to enter our shelter, and in making that entrance, we introduce a weak spot into our safe space. This necessary balancing act—safety versus access—has led to thresholds being treated as dangerous spaces that require extra magickal warding. As it was in the past, so it is today.

For the purpose of this section, the threshold will pertain not only to any doors that allow access to a home from the outside but also to any doors or doorways that mark a boundary between the private and the public. If you share your home with roommates or housemates, you can treat the door between your bedroom and the communal rooms as a threshold and guard it accordingly.

The point is not to take a paranoid view of the outside world as a perilous realm that must be kept at bay. Recognizing thresholds and warding them is as necessary as having a lock on your front door. You are not only protecting your home, but you are delineating your space and giving a heads up to the genius loci and any other spirits that it is your space. It helps avoid any confusion.

EXERCISE
Keeping It Neat and Tidy

The entry to your home shouldn't present an obstacle to those who are allowed in. This means keeping the entry clear of clutter. No piles of shoes and coats on the floor, no umbrellas or walking sticks leaning against the door, no rug askew to trip you on your way in and out.

Look at your entryway and see what you can do to keep it uncluttered and clear. Consider the usual traffic, both in and out. What do people need when they come in? A place to hang their coat? A place for shoes? Is there a place to put keys, your wallet, or whatever else you need when you go out?

Once you've assessed your needs, set about addressing them. Perhaps a basket for shoes, a valet for keys, a stand for umbrellas and canes. Something as simple as a wooden kitchen chair set by the door to provide a place for a bag and coat, with a space beneath for your shoes, will help keep the clutter to a minimum. Your goals are twofold: (1) to create an area that allows ease of entrance and exit and (2) to have a place for everything.

Finally, when you have created an entryway that is practical, you must get in the habit of using it as you have set it up. The hook on the wall isn't going to be helpful if you toss your coat onto the couch. If you have set up your entryway in such a way that fits your own life patterns then it should be simple to use it how you intended. If it isn't, if you find yourself struggling to remember where your keys are because you forget to drop them in the box by the door, then you'll need to reassess your setup.

Keep in mind, as well, that if you live with others you'll want to take their individual needs and traits into consideration. And once you have set everything up, you'll need to explain it to everyone who lives there. Don't assume it will be apparent to everyone. Children, especially, will need clear direction, and it might take them a bit to get used to storing their shoes in the cubby instead of just kicking them off at the door.

It can even be a beneficial exercise to have your family help in setting up the entryway or to at least get their input. Doing so can foster bonds, strengthen your relationships, and bolster the feeling that the home belongs to everyone.

Environmental Concerns

The world around us contains so much more than we experience. Genius loci, elemental forces, deities, ghosts, and much more will share the same space as us, though it may not be on the same plane. Especially in places where there has been a lot of turmoil, the area can be host to various entities. Some won't pay you any mind, others might watch you curiously, and a smaller portion might actually object to your presence. It is wise to keep any resident spirits in mind as you live, work, and play. They have most likely been there before you showed up and will remain long after you are gone.

Start by learning about the land you live on. What are the local legends? Who lived here before, meaning who were the indigenous peoples? Who has since moved into, moved out of, or is still settled in the area? What nationalities and cultures shaped the way the neighborhood grew? Immigrants will have brought their own spirits with them along with their cuisine and language, and some of those spirits will have taken up residence, even staying after the makeup of the population has shifted. Other factors, such as gentrification, will have an effect on the spiritual landscape.

Once you've done your research, set about introducing yourself to the genius loci. You are not trying to contact them (again, they might not care, and if they mean you harm, you don't want to talk to them anyway). Just a simple introduction will suffice. If any local spirits want further contact, they'll let you know. Even if you've lived in your home for years, you should make the introduction. Politeness can go a long way to smoothing over any negative feelings.

Spells to Protect Your Home

The spells provided here are all meant to be companions and used in conjunction with other safety measures. They are not meant to replace precautions like locking doors and windows. The witch utilizes every means at their disposal to accomplish a goal: that means not only warding their home against robbery, but also using alarm systems, smoke detectors, and other security measures.

The spells that follow focus on protection from physical harm as well as magickal and psychic harm. Whether an attack is purposeful (as in someone is hexing you) or unintended (some variations of the evil eye aren't directed and are cast unwittingly) doesn't matter if you suffer ill effects. At the bare minimum, you should have a talisman hung at your door to protect the entrance in and out.

When bad things happen, one of your first actions should be to renew any wards or protective spells. If that doesn't stop the trouble, use a divination technique you are comfortable with to pinpoint the origin of the problem.

Boundary Protection Spell

Protective barriers are like underwear: they should be refreshed often. Because of that I prefer to keep such spells simple and straightforward. All you need for this one is your visualization and a crystal or herb or other item that has protective energies. See the table on page 60 if you want ideas.

Take your chosen protective materia magica in hand and stand near your threshold. Close your eyes and extend your consciousness outward to the boundary of your home. If you live in a detached house, you will visualize the outside of it. If you live in an apartment, condo, or other place that shares walls with other structures, you are going to visualize just inside your walls, behind the drywall to where the frame is. You don't want your protection to extend into your neighbor's home because that is not your space and you'll be intruding. Also, if your neighbor has protections of their own, the two could interfere with each other. Whatever your living situation, you want to visualize the boundary of your home.

Once you have the image clear in your mind's eye, you are going to draw up the energy from your protective focus as well as draw on your own personal energy. As you breathe in, pull up the two, visualizing them as two cords made of light, both different colors. Breathe out, exhaling the two energies into your home's boundaries. You may see this as a layer of light imbuing the walls or a dome erecting over your home. It may even appear to you as if you are knitting a cozy that wraps around the exterior. However you visualize it, continue breathing in and drawing on the energy and then breathing out and exhaling it into your protective barrier.

See this barrier encompassing the entire home, both at floor level and up to the ceiling or over the roof. If the home has a basement, make sure that space is enclosed. Once you have completed the barrier, charge it by saying, "No magick, no entity, nothing that means me or mine ill can cross this boundary, so I will it." Stop the flow of energy from you and your protective focus. Ground any excess magickal energy, open your eyes, and go on your way.

This spell, once you have mastered it, should take no longer than a minute or two. You don't have to use the same materia magica every time, either. In fact you may find that certain materials work better for you than others, or you might want to coordinate your protective focus with different concerns. Look through the table that follows and experiment until you are completely at ease with the spell.

Protective Materia Magica

The following items can be used in the Boundary Protection Spell. Stones, plant material, and symbols can be held, and scents can be inhaled. You can also use a tone, such as ringing a bell, as your spell component, drawing the magickal protective energy from the sound. Feel free to combine items as well, such as using a heart carved from smoky quartz or an iron dragon statuette.

Crystals/ Stones	Herbs	Scents	Symbols	Animals
Black tourmaline	Bay leaf	Basil	Pentacle	Snake
Jet	Carnation	Cinnamon	Heart	Owl
Fluorite	Clover	Clove	Triple Moon	Wolf
Obsidian	Fleabane	Coconut	Hecate's wheel	Dragon
Amethyst	Marigold	Mint	Horseshoe	Unicorn
Labradorite	Mugwort	Lavender	Iron nail	Bee
Smoky quartz	Oak	Pine	Eye	Dog
Carnelian	Rice	Rose	Sun	Cat

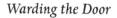

Warding the Door

You lock the door to keep out unwelcome visitors, and it should be warded to keep any spirits or metaphysical harm from entering your home. There are countless folk magic methods to ward and protect a threshold, from driving a nail into the doorframe, to hanging rowan branches over the lintel. Every culture has a way to protect the entrance. You can spend a lot of time exploring various folk practices from your familial culture to find a ward that speaks to you and works with your life. If you don't know your cultural magickal roots, or if you are estranged from that history, you can use the technique in the following paragraph.

Use the Hestia oil from page 50. With the thumb or the index finger of your dominant hand, mark the door and windows either outside or inside with the oil. You can either just mark a dot or draw a symbol (a circle, an equilateral cross, etc.) on the surface. As you do so, say, "Hestia, protect this home from all harm—intentional or no; physical, magickal, or other; whether it comes from within or without." Repeat this twice a year on the winter and summer solstices, and recharge more often if you feel the need.

Other ways you can ward your doors include drawing a line of salt before the door or just inside the doorway. You can set statues to stand guard inside and out of the door. Garden statues such as gargoyles and lions are readily available, but you can also choose smaller statues for inside. Owl statues that are set out to discourage woodpeckers can be charmed to act as protective guardians as well.

Protective Door Talisman

The following talisman is hung over the door on the inside of the home. It acts as a protective shield, keeping out unwanted and harmful spirits, energies, magick, emotions, and the like.

For this talisman you'll need the following items:

Dime minted before 1965

Dried bay leaves

Pen

1 teaspoon of sea, kosher, or rock salt

Frankincense or sandalwood incense, or dried rosemary and a charcoal disc

Small pouch

Optional: An apotropaic symbol, such as a pentacle, nazar (an eye-shaped amulet), fascinum (an amulet featuring a phallus), etc.

Yellow ribbon or piece of string or yarn

You want to use a dime minted before 1965, as that is the year the metal composition of the dime was changed by the US Mint. Before 1965, dimes were made up of 90 percent silver. Afterward, silver was removed from the mixture, and they are now minted from a mixture of copper and nickel. Silver as a metal has protective properties. It will reflect harm back on the sender.

Bay leaves are magickally protective as well. You'll be writing the names of all the people who live in your home and who are to be protected by the talisman on the leaf (if it is big enough) or on individual leaves. You want the writing to last, so test out a few different types of pen until you find one that works beforehand.

In this talisman the salt works as a trap, soaking up any non-targeted harm that might try to enter the house or that might be clinging to people entering the home. This is one spell where using rock salt can be useful, as larger crystals are easier to clean out when you need to recharge your talisman.

Create your talisman during a full moon. You can inscribe the bay leaf (or leaves) ahead of time. Burn an incense of frankincense or sandalwood (both used for cleansing and consecration), or burn dried rosemary on a charcoal disc. Smoke cleanse your pouch and the spell components by holding them briefly in the incense smoke. This is going to cleanse them of any energies that may already be clinging to them. This is especially important for the pouch and dime, as they are the items most likely to have been handled by others.

Hold the pouch in your receptive hand. Say (or think), "Talisman, I create you to protect this home."

Place the bay leaf (or leaves) into the pouch and say (or think), "Talisman, I task you with protecting those who dwell in this home."

Place the dime in the pouch and say (or think), "Talisman, I task you to reflect back to the sender any and all harm that is directed against this home."

Add the salt into the pouch and say (or think), "Talisman, I task you to soak up and stop any harm that might try to enter this home."

You can add whatever other apotropaic symbols or charms to the pouch that you might desire. Then say (or think), "Hestia, I ask you to lend your aid in charging this talisman." You can also call on any helper spirits, ancestors, deities, or other entities you may want to help with the spell. Wait a moment to give your supernatural allies time to direct their energies into the bag.

Now hold your dominant hand over the pouch and activate the talisman by charging it with your own magickal energy. See it flowing from the palm of your hand into the bag. You don't need much.

Tie the pouch shut with the ribbon or string. Say, aloud or in your head, "Talisman, I set you to your task. Protect this home and all who dwell within it." Hang the talisman above the door.

The salt will need to be changed out every so often, at least twice a year. You can recharge the talisman when you do so. Take down the pouch and empty out the contents. Dispose of the old salt and add the new. Recharge it with your own energy before you close the pouch and rehang it.

If the string or fabric ever breaks or if the talisman ever falls from its place for an undiscovered reason (it wasn't bumped down or the nail you hung it on didn't fall out), this means that it has repelled a targeted magickal attack. You'll need to create a new talisman. Bury the old, damaged one at either a crossroads or a place far from your home.

Rituals

Moving into a New Home

When you are moving into a space, before you have started to bring in your furniture and boxes, take an hour to perform a ritual to only bless your new home.

For the following ritual, you will need:

Candle

Water

Salt

Bells

Oil

Bread

Light the candle and carry it throughout the house, to each room. In each room sprinkle the water and salt in the corners. Shake the bells. As you do this, visualize all old, negative energies, any unwelcome spirits, and any lingering magicks or intentions being driven off. You are clearing out the space, setting it to a blank, neutral state so that you can settle in. When you do this, leave a window or door open so that the energies you are moving have a way to leave.

Once the home is cleared out, set your mark upon it. Using oil, draw an X, a circle, a sigil, a rune, or whatever symbol you feel is appropriate over the door on the outside. Repeat on any door that leads to the outside. You are not only laying claim to your new home but letting all the genius loci know you are there.

Finish the ritual by laying out an offering of bread or some other foodstuff as a gesture of goodwill to the genius loci. Introduce yourself, aloud or in your head, to your new neighbors. Assure them you mean no harm, let them know you are there to stay, and invite them to get to know you (if you wish to work with the local spirits) or assure them that you will stay out of their way.

Lighting the Hearth

In ancient days, the first fire of a new community or house would be lit from the fire of an existing fire. This provided an unbroken lineage from the ancestral fire to the new one, establishing the new hearth as part of the community. The tradition served a practical purpose as well, in a day when kindling a fire wasn't as simple as striking a match.

These days it's not really practical to carry literal fire from one place to another, unless you are moving in easy walking distance. If you would like to keep the lineage between your old home and new, if, say you are moving from your childhood home out on your own or you are establishing a new home with another person, there are a few ways to do so that keep the spirit of the practice alive.

1. Anoint a candle in the home you are moving from. Draw a bit of the sense of the place into the candle by envisioning a happy memory you have of the place and affixing it to the candle. Then, when you get to your new home, burn the candle to release that sense of happiness and comfort into your space.

2. Bring matches or a lighter from the previous home to light a candle in your new space, or have a member of the previous household be the one to light the candle in your new place.

3. Light a candle in the old space. Let it burn an inch or so, then snuff it. Take the candle to the new place and light it, lighting new candles from it and letting it burn all the way down.

If you are moving away from a place where you were abused, were neglected, didn't feel safe, or were otherwise not comfortable, don't bring that energy with you to your new place. Smoke cleanse or otherwise cleanse yourself before you enter your new home. Use scissors to cut any ties that might bind you to the old place. Scatter protective herbs in front of your door to repel any negativity that might try to follow you.

On Leaving the Home, on Returning to the Home

Leaving home means exiting safety and going out into the potential unknown. Returning means leaving behind the outside world, if only for a while. These are activities that we engage in multiple times a day, which make them perfect for creating ritual.

Rituals are a way to bring order and meaning to our day and activities. The rituals you create will serve two functions. First, they will help you get in the right frame of mind. Second, they help in delineating what is your safe space and what is not. This is an important distinction to have. When you cast spells to target your home or to keep harmful entities out, you need to have a feel for what that space actually is.

A ritual leaving the house can be as simple as touching the threshold when you leave and when you return. I have a string of turtle beads that hang over the light switch that serve as such a "touchstone," which I touch the fingers of my right hand to when I leave the house. Returning means you are entering a space of safety. It can involve touching the threshold or the doorknob and inwardly recognizing that you have entered sacred space. This is especially effective if your home is limited to a room within a building or house. You can designate a spot as your touchstone, using the Hestia oil to mark the spot. When you leave your room or house, touch the spot and say to yourself, "I am leaving home." When you return, touch the spot and say to yourself, "I have returned home."

If you have placed statues outside your home as metaphysical protectors, you can take to saying goodbye to them, charging them to guard the home while you are gone as you leave. When you return home, you then thank them for having done so. The same can be done if your home hosts any household spirits you are in contact with.

You can use sound by ringing a bell when you leave and return. You can light a candle on your altar when you are home and snuff it when you leave. Whatever you decide on, the key is to perform the ritual consistently. If you find yourself forgetting, it might be a good idea to create a different ritual.

Claiming Space

As a woman, I've been conditioned not to take up too much space. As, kids we're supposed to be seen, not heard. Girls are told not to roughhouse or horse around, to be quiet and ladylike. Women are told their place is in the kitchen while men are said to be the king of their castle. This attitude that tells men to take up space and women to shrink themselves down is harmful to creating a healthy home.

I encourage those of you who have been on the receiving end of such limiting talk to take the time to claim your space, even if you've lived in your home for years, even if you only have one room that is truly yours.

If you are part of a group—family or otherwise—that is going to perform a formal ritual to claim your home, give care to make sure all members are participating to the extent that they are comfortable. It's always a good idea to confront what you are doing, to interrogate your actions and intentions for any biased thinking and conditioning. Especially with respect to ritual.

All you need for this ritual is a song you really love, one that moves you. Turn on the music and dance through your home. Sing along with the music at the top of your lungs. Go from room to room, making sure you dance in every one. If the idea of dancing makes you feel self-conscious, you can close your blinds and curtains. If you are worried about disturbing the neighbors, wear headphones and perform the ritual during the daytime. It doesn't matter if you have no rhythm—you aren't going to be judged on your skills as a dancer. You are asserting your right to be in the space you are living in.

If you are doing this ritual with your family, make sure to pick a song that everyone loves. And dance with your family. Hold hands and twirl each other around. Dip your loved one in an exaggerated ballroom maneuver. This ritual is the polar opposite of a somber ritual. This is meant to be fun and joyful and silly.

Repeat this ritual as often as needed. There is no right or wrong time to do it.

5

THE KITCHEN: LOVE AND TRANSFORMATION

While the image of a cauldron bubbling over a fire in a one-room cottage is familiar, kitchens were historically often built away from the main house for reasons of safety and comfort (the heat from kitchen fires wouldn't be welcome during the hot summer months). In fact, the kitchen as the hearth and heart of a home is a rather modern invention based as much on recent divisions of labor between men and women as on the introduction of the stove into the home. The hearth in many of our ancestors' homes wasn't used for cooking but for warmth and light.

A village might only have one oven, available for use to others. In fact, certain cooking tasks, such as baking, might have only been undertaken by professionals. So if you can't even boil water without setting off the smoke detector, don't fret. Cooking is a skill not everyone has cultivated, and there's no shame in that. The point of this section is not kitchen witchery or even cooking (that topic is covered later in chapter 9).

One of the first acts of love we experience is being fed. The connection between food and love is encoded in our language, from claiming "the way to a man's heart is through his stomach" to calling someone the "apple of my eye." We cook and eat comfort food and have romantic dinners. Advertisers tell us that eating together is what makes a family in their bid to get us to buy meal kits or eat at restaurants.

Magick makes the connection as well. The love potion is an idea so familiar that it has become almost a cliché in modern media and entertainment. But it has its roots in witchcraft, and many traditional folk magick love spells required feeding the object of one's affection to work.

As a virgin goddess who actively spurned marriage, Hestia isn't the goddess you turn to for help with your dating life. And so, when working with her, the love we want to promote is familial, rather than sexual or romantic.

Crafts

Smoke Cleansing Bundles

Many of the smoke cleansing bundles sold commercially are made from white sage or sweet grass and marketed as smudge sticks. This is problematic on a number of levels, which you can read about in the section "Cultural Appropriation: What It Is and How Not to Do It" on page 195. Instead of adding to the problem, you can create your own smoke cleansing bundles. They aren't difficult to make and they allow you to choose herbs that are suited to your particular needs.

Start by choosing one of the following herbs: mugwort, rosemary, thyme, or lavender. All four have magickal properties of cleansing and purification. You want fresh sprigs of the herb. Make sure there is no moisture lingering on the sprigs. If not, you could end up with mold ruining your bundle.

You will need:

    Paper

    Pen

Your chosen herb in sprigs 8 inches long

Heavy cotton thread in black or white

Scissors

1. Start by writing the date and the name of the herb, along with its magickal uses, on a piece of paper. Bundles of dried herbs can look alike at times, especially if you have several.

2. Bundle together the herbs.

3. Cut a piece of cotton thread 24 inches in length.

4. Tie a loop at one end of the thread. Wrap the thread around one end of the bundle, threading the straight end of the thread through the loop and pulling it tight.

5. Wrap the thread down the bundle, pulling it tight. When you get to the end of the bundle, wrap the thread back toward

where you started. Tie the thread ends together. Attach the note from step 1 to the thread ends.

6. Hang the bundle from a shelf or hook where it can dry. Ensure there is air flow around the entire bundle. Let dry for 2 to 3 weeks.

Infused Oil for Cooking

One of the most basic ways to bring energies of peace and love into your cooking is to start with your ingredients. Many recipes call for oil for cooking or flavoring a dish. Take advantage of that by creating infused oils for cooking using the instructions on page 48.

You will need ¾ cup of extra-virgin olive oil and a bundle of herbs or peel from the following table.

Intention	Ingredients	Culinary Use
To inspire friendship	Lemon peel (make sure to remove as much as the pith— white inner peel— as possible before use)	Use in salad dressings or drizzle on steamed broccoli or on pasta.
To inspire love	Rosemary and thyme, 1 bundle fresh or 1 teaspoon dried each	Pour 2 tablespoons of the oil into a shallow dish, add a sprinkling of parmesan cheese, and serve as a dip for bread.

Intention	Ingredients	Culinary Use
For general protection	2 cloves garlic, 1 teaspoon dried peppercorns	Mix 3 tablespoons of oil with ½ cup of softened butter and a tablespoon of chopped parsley. Spread on 2 halves of a french loaf and bake for 8 to 10 minutes in a 400-degree Fahrenheit oven for garlic bread.

Make sure that the fresh herbs or peels you use are completely dry when you start. If water gets into the process, the oil can become moldy and unsafe to use in cooking. You can use dried herbs for the oil. In that case you will only need a teaspoon or so of the dried, crushed herb, rather than a bundle.

After you have infused the oil and stored it in a glass bottle, you can add a fresh sprig to the bottle (again, make sure it is completely dried). Not only is this pretty to look at, but it can help you keep track of which oil is which if you decide to make more than one to keep on hand.

Placemats

Placemats can feel like an antiquated concept—an extra piece of fabric that only adds to the workload of housekeeping. Let me offer three counterarguments. Placemats protect tables from water rings and scorching from cups and hot plates, respectively. Second, they help with cleanup, catching spilled food. Finally, placemats provide a ready-made vessel for magick.

The instructions below require minimal sewing skills. They have been written to reduce fabric waste and will give you four placemats when you have finished. Choose a heavy-weight fabric like canvas, denim, or twill. Take the opportunity to express your creativity through your choice of fabric color or pattern.

You can imbue your placemat with loving energies by adding a sigil, rune, or symbol to the fabric. My preference is for a simple hand-drawn heart. If you have a personal sign for love, use that.

You will need:

> 1 yard of fabric
>
> Scissors
>
> Your loving symbol
>
> Red pencil
>
> Coordinating thread
>
> Sewing machine (or sewing needle if sewing by hand)
>
> Steam iron

1. Cut the fabric into eight 18 × 14½-inch rectangles.

2. On the wrong side of 4 of the fabric rectangles, draw your loving symbol with the red pencil. As you do so, think about the loving relationships in your life, the people you share meals with, those who cook for you, and those you share your love with. Channel the affection you feel for them into the symbol.

3. Pair up the fabric, 1 marked and 1 unmarked piece. With their right sides facing, sew the front and back sides together. Use a ½-inch seam allowance. Leave a 3-inch gap for turning.

4. Clip the corners. Trim the seams.

5. Turn the placemat right side out. Push out the corners with a chopstick or skewer. Press with the steam iron.

6. Sew ⅛ inch from the edge around all sides of the placemat.

Napkins

Cloth napkins provide you with one of the best ways to reduce your paper product consumption. More than that, however, using the napkins, especially in conjunction with placements, elevates dining to more of an occasion than simply gaining nutrients.

You don't need fancy linen for these napkins. Muslin or broadcloth work just as well for a fraction of the cost. Before you start sewing, wash the fabric to preshrink it. This keeps the napkins from puckering out of shape later. The instructions below make four napkins.

You can bring magick into your napkins through your choice of fabric and thread color. White wards off doubts and fears, bringing peace to your table. Orange pulls things to you and carries energy of the harvest, bringing all the fruits of your labor to your plate. Blue promotes domestic harmony. Pink and red have loving energies. Brown corresponds with practicality and sound decision-making, should you need some of that in your life.

You will need:

> 1 yard of fabric
>
> Scissors
>
> Thread
>
> Sewing machine (or sewing needle if sewing by hand)
>
> Steam iron

1. Cut four 18 × 18-inch squares from the fabric.
2. Fold one edge of the fabric up ½ inch along the entire length. Press. Fold it again another ½ inch and press. Repeat with the side opposite. Now repeat for the remaining two sides.
3. On the right side of the napkin, stitch around all four sides, close to the edge of the first fold.

Spells

Salt and Pepper Shaker Charms

Both salt and pepper have magickal protective properties. When you season your food, take advantage of that. Charm the shakers and their contents to keep negativity out of your food when you season it. They can help protect from illness related to food (heart disease, indigestion, food poisoning) as well as psychological or emotional illness (eating disorders, unhealthy attitudes toward eating, etc.).

Spell Bundles

Toilet paper rolls are one of those ubiquitous pieces of garbage that can be put to magickal use. Rather than throwing them out, reuse them as containers for spell bundles. Decorate the outside with sigils, runes, symbols, and drawings. Fill them with herbs, resins, and slips of paper bearing intentions and prayers. Then anoint the bundle and burn or bury it as you require.

To close your bundles and keep everything from spilling out, slightly flatten the tube at the beginning. This also makes it easier to decorate the outside. At one end, push one side in and then the other. Repeat on the other end. You will be left with a package that looks like a fancy gift box. If it helps, view these bundles as presents you are giving the universe, filled with your magick and your will to change things.

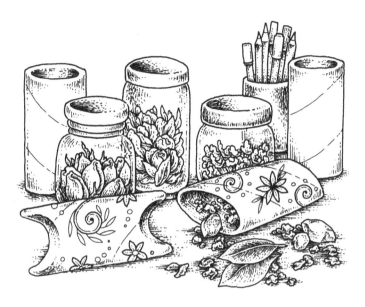

If you are going to burn your spell bundle, make sure not to overfill it. Otherwise, the flames will just snuff out and you'll be left with a half-burned magickal present. For those without access to a fireplace, spell bundles can be burned on grills or even in a large fireproof container. They should only be burned out of doors if not in a fireplace to avoid setting off smoke detectors and any possibility of the fire spreading.

Transitioning Spell Bundle

Fire is the element of transformation, and this bundle takes advantage of that association to aid trans people who are transitioning. The fire burns away the outer shell (the toilet paper roll) that represents the view the world outside has seen up to now and reveals the real person. Burn your bundle during a new moon.

You will need:

>   Colored pencils, pens, or markers
>
>   Empty toilet paper roll
>
>   1 tablespoon each of dried peppermint and spearmint
>
>   Bay leaf
>
>   Piece of Picasso jasper

Decorate the outside of the empty toilet paper roll with symbols of change, your deadname, the pronouns you had to use, and anything else that represents what you are shedding and leaving behind.

Both peppermint and spearmint have magickal energies of success, happiness, and transformation. Mix the two herbs together. Add 1 tablespoon to the spell bundle. Bay leaf has magickal properties of healing, strength, and transformation. On the leaf write your name in your favorite color. Add it to the spell bundle. Picasso jasper is a stone that provides support during change and transformation. Place the stone in the bundle. Add the rest of the dried mint herb mix to the spell bundle and close it.

Before you burn the spell bundle, hold it in your hands and charge it with your personal energy. Burn the bundle, making sure that every flammable component is consumed. As it burns, see yourself as the phoenix, emerging anew from the ashes. Once the spell bundle has burned completely and the ashes have cooled, retrieve the Picasso jasper. Carry it with you to sustain you and provide protection as you go out into the world.

Love Candle Spell

Kindle the warmth of familial love with this candle spell. While the wax is poured into lemon halves, you should place them on heat-proof dishes when burning. Burn these candles during family gatherings, especially ones that include eating. The lemon, rosemary, and thyme will add energies of love and blessing into the space. The beeswax binds their energies together and brings properties of community to the spell. The coconut oil helps keep the beeswax from burning too quickly and adds a lovely scent to the air.

You will need:

    1 medium-size lemon

    2 cups water

    1 ounce beeswax

    1 teaspoon each of dried rosemary and thyme

    1 ounce coconut oil

    Wood toothpicks

1. Slice the lemon in half lengthwise and remove the insides. Shave a small bit off of the bottom of each halves if needed so they sit level. Set the empty halves aside.

2. Fill a saucepan with 2 cups of water. Place a smaller pan into the saucepan. Make sure the water does not get into the smaller pan.

3. Add the beeswax to the smaller pan and heat the water until it is just boiling. Melt the beeswax.

4. Add the coconut oil to the melted beeswax and stir until it has melted and the two have combined.

5. Poke a toothpick into the center of each lemon half.

6. Pour the wax and oil into each half, carefully, making sure not to overfill it.

7. Sprinkle the dried rosemary and thyme into the wax while it is still hot.

8. Let the wax cool.

Rituals

Setting the Table Ritual

Mealtimes, especially dinner, can often be the only time in the day that everyone in a family is together. If that is the case in your home, make the most of it. Take the time to ask everyone how their day has been going, perhaps even making it a habit to go around the table to give people a chance to speak. Encourage active listening among everyone there so the people feel heard. Go so far as to ban phones from the table. Mealtime will be over soon enough, and people will scatter to their separate spaces once again.

When setting the table, take the opportunity to invite more than just your family to eat. As you place the plates and bowls, the napkins and utensils, say, "Peace is nurtured at this table. Love is nurtured at this table. Harmony is nurtured at this table." See peace, love, and harmony settling over the table. These are gentle energies that will seep into the dishes, into the table and chairs, into the napkins, and so on.

After dinner is over, and as you clear away the dishes, thank the energies of peace, love, and harmony for joining you. These aren't necessarily entities, but it doesn't hurt to show gratitude for their presence.

Gratitude Ritual

Expressing gratitude is a ritual that tends to be limited to holidays like Thanksgiving, when people sit at the table and have to say what they are thankful for before they can eat. That can sour people on the idea of giving thanks. When times are tough, it can be challenging to count our blessings because they are harder to see through the difficulties.

Researchers have looked into gratitude and found that when we give thanks we reap plenty of benefits. People who can pinpoint things they appreciate on a regular basis have reported being happier and more optimistic. And those relationships in which the partners tell each other thank you regularly see better communication. It appears that *thank you* are as much the magick words as *please* in this case.

To practice gratitude regularly, and to encourage the others in your family to do the same, invest in some refrigerator poetry magnets or a wipe board that you can attach to your fridge. Every day use the magnets to create a statement of gratitude, or write it on the wipe board. Have others do the same. Seeing how a refrigerator door is opened between fifteen and twenty times a day, that is fifteen to twenty times a day to be exposed to your expression of gratitude.

Fire Gazing

Fire gazing is a form of scrying that involves staring into the flames or embers of a fire and interpreting the visions you see. If you don't have access to a fire, you can use candles instead.

Improve your divination skills by burning herbs such as dandelion, goldenrod, marigold, or mugwort in the fire or as loose incense, or by dressing candles with thyme or orange oils. You can invite Hestia to join you. As a fire goddess, she has plenty of experience of reading the flames. Before you start the actual scrying, make sure to center and ground yourself.

To start, build your fire. Sit near the fire where you will be comfortable, neither too warm nor too cold. Look into the flames and let your gaze go soft, unfocused. Think about the question at hand, then look for images in the flame. Don't strain. Scry for about five minutes and then close your eyes. Use your intuition to interpret the images that came to you.

If you are using a candle for your fire gazing, you can choose a color related to your question: red for relationships, green for money, purple for goals, and so on. Or you can stick to a white candle. Light the candle and darken the room. Sit so that the candle is at eye level. Just as with a fire, let your gaze soften as you stare at the flame. Don't spend more than five minutes at a time staring at the flame.

6

THE LIVING ROOM:
COMMUNICATION AND FRIENDSHIP

Called by a variety of names throughout the centuries—parlor, drawing room, family room, and many more—the living room at one point in time was the only room in a house. People would work, socialize, bathe, eat, sleep, and live in the one room. As houses changed, other functions were separated from the main room into their own special chambers. What was left was a room that was a catchall for those activities that didn't belong to cooking or eating or bathing or sleeping. Every other part of living happened there.

And now, after splitting everything apart, relegating, and categorizing those activities, there's been a movement in housebuilding to see a reconciliation between the different living spaces. Open floor planning crops up time and again in various house models. We should be able to see into the kitchen, dining room, study, formal dining room, and all those other spaces from the living room. This open airiness aims at bringing back a sense of an earlier time when we did our living together.

The living room is ruled by the air element. It is here that we entertain not only others but ourselves. In many households the living or family room has taken over as the "heart" of the home, where we gather to feel connected. It is where we share ideas and are exposed to new concepts through the television, books, and the newspaper.

This is a room of comfort. We fill it with sofas and easy chairs, pillows and throws, all meant to encourage us to take our ease. It is where we gather with friends and family to watch sporting events or play games. It is often where we place our seasonal decorations to mark the Wheel of the Year. In my own home it is where our family altar is so that everyone can make use of it.

In this section we explore spells and rituals relating to communication and ideas, to friendship and community. You might be surprised to find houseplants and flowers featuring so heavily here, as they fall under the domain of the earth element. However, I've always found that most houseplants are kept in the living room, thanks to the number of windows found there compared to other rooms in the house.

Magickal Houseplants

I dream of the time when I will be able to fill my home with enough plants to qualify it as a small, localized jungle. Growing up, houseplants were everywhere, not only in my home but those of my grandmother and aunts. I can still recall the planters: mostly terra-cotta and ceramic, as well the occasional plastic flowerpot, and even reused food containers. Weekend chores were never complete until we had watered all the plants, going from room to room with the pitcher that usually held iced tea or lemonade but had been conscripted to watering duty Saturday mornings.

The importance of houseplants is so firmly ingrained in me that my typical housewarming gift is whiskey, a loaf of homemade bread, and a plant. The gift of a houseplant is a sacred act, and with so many that are easy to maintain (such as golden pothos or a cactus), it doesn't have to involve any anxiety over keeping the gift alive.

Houseplants provide benefits beyond beauty. NASA did studies on plants and air quality in the 1980s and concluded that plants could provide natural filters for chemicals such as formaldehyde, benzene, and trichloroethylene.[16] Other plants have scents that aid in relaxation and sleep. Still others, such as aloe vera, have health and first aid uses that make them helpful to have around the house.

Many plants have common names that reference animals, minerals, and so on (for example, spider plant). Look to these as clues to what deeper magickal uses the plant may hold. Also the color of the leaves and flowers, as well as the number of petals, can be consulted for magickal properties.

16. B. C. Wolverton, Willard L. Douglas, and Keith Bounds, "A Study of Interior Landscape Plants for Indoor Air Pollution Abatement," NASA, July 1989.

Place the plants on your altar or in your circle or the space where you will be casting a spell to include their energy in your spellwork. Place crystals, magick tools, tarot and oracle cards, and the like near plants to charge them with the particular magickal properties of the plant.

Some houseplants are toxic if ingested. If you have pets or small children, it is important to keep those plants out of the reach of them. Plants that are toxic have been marked in their entry.

Any and all of these plants can be placed in your living room space to encourage relaxation and remove negativity. Some of the plants detailed below are also suited to specific rooms, such as the bedroom. As long as you have the space and the adequate light, scatter the plants around your house, especially those that have protective magickal qualities to expand that protection throughout your home.

African Violet (**Saintpaulia ionantha**)

When I was growing up, there was always a small African violet in the kitchen windowsill, right next to green tomatoes left to ripen in the summer. African violets are not toxic to pets. They can provide blooms during those seasons when the earth outside has gone dormant.

The African violet originated in eastern tropical Africa. It is associated with the goddess Aphrodite (Venus) and with the element of water. The five petals of African violet flowers tap into all the magickal properties of the number five, especially its correspondence to marriage and love. Additionally, the bluish and purplish leaves tap into the properties of those hues, such as health, communication, and peace. African violets have protective magickal properties and symbolize admiration, connections, and faithfulness.

African violets need light for about twelve hours a day and eight hours of dark to bloom. Bright indirect light is best. Water when the soil is dry to touch and use room temperature water. Keep in a room with moderate temperature and humidity. Remove dead flowers to encourage new blooms.

Air Plant (Tillandsia)

Air plants have always fascinated me, as their spiky appearance gives them a slight otherworldliness. As the name suggests, air plants obtain nutrients and water from the air around them, and their roots serve only to anchor them to rock or wood. Because of this, any number of items can serve as a holder for an air plant—from wine corks to crystals.

Air plants are native to the West Indies, Mexico, and Central and South America. Unsurprisingly, they are associated with the element of air. They symbolize freedom and creativity.

Air plants are low maintenance. While they do not require watering, arid conditions are not good for the plants. This combined with their preference for a high-light environment means they'll need the occasional misting to supplement what water can be gotten from the inside air.

Aloe Vera (Aloe vera)

Every single household I knew growing up had at least one aloe plant. It was kept on hand for its skin soothing properties. I recall once when my mother spilled a casserole full of rice down her front. The sprawling, years-old aloe that dominated the dining room cabinet was thrown into the blender and the resulting slurry used to help ease the burns she suffered.

Aloe originates from the Arabian Peninsula. It is associated with the moon and the element of water. It has magickal properties of protection and luck, and it symbolizes healing and protection. A potted aloe vera can be placed near a window so that its spiky leaves can impale any dangers that might make it into your home.

Aloe vera likes bright indirect sunlight. Water when the top one or two inches of the soil are dry. Letting the soil dry between waterings keeps the roots from rotting.

Lucky Bamboo (**Dracaena sanderiana**)

Despite the name, lucky bamboo is not truly bamboo. It actually belongs to the asparagus family, although it superficially resembles the actual bamboo (which, incidentally, is not actually a tree, but a type of grass, which I feel is some trickster-god-level chicanery).

Lucky bamboo is native to Central Africa. It is used in feng shui with the number of stalks having a specific purpose, such as three stalks for love and marriage or eight stalks for wealth and abundance. Feng shui also instructs where to place your bamboo to affect certain aspects of your life. Consult a book on feng shui to learn more. It has magickal properties of good luck and fortune.

Lucky bamboo likes bright light. It is often potted in a container of water, which should be replaced every couple of months (or if the water becomes cloudy or foul smelling). Water to keep the roots covered. Also rotate the plant so that all sides get evenly sunned.

Cacti (**Cactaceae** *spp.*)

The cactus is one of the few houseplants that has an immense variety of shapes, sizes, and colors to work with. It is one of those plants that can handle neglect to a degree as well, which makes it suitable for those who aren't very flora-inclined.

Cacti are native to the Americas (with the exception of one species that is found in Africa and Sri Lanka). They have magickal properties of protection, especially "against unwanted intrusions and burglaries."[17] They symbolize endurance and thriving despite hardship. Cactus spines can be used in protective spells and talismans. Like the aloe vera, placing cacti near or in windows provides natural magickal protection.

Cacti like bright light. They should be rotated once a month to ensure even light. Underwatering is better than overwatering, so watering once a month is sufficient.

Cyclamen (**Cyclamen** *spp.*)

Cyclamen is another flowering houseplant. The leaves range from round to heart-shaped. The upper leaves have various shades of green and silver, while the underside coloring varies from green to purple. Varieties of cyclamen bloom in different seasons, meaning you could have flowers throughout the year. Flower color can be white, pink, or purple. Blooms have five petals and are cup shaped.

The cyclamen that are grown as houseplants originate from Persia (present-day Iran). Magickally, they have powers of fertility, protection, happiness, and lust. Cunningham suggests placing a plant in the bedroom to protect sleepers.[18] It can be used in love spells. It symbolizes sincere and lasting feelings, making it a great gift to loved ones.

Cyclamen are the Goldilocks of plants: they want everything to be just right. That means they don't like cool temperatures (anything under 40 degrees Fahrenheit) or exceedingly hot temperatures. With regard to watering, they don't want sopping wet soil, nor do they want to dry out. When soil is dry to touch, water thoroughly and make sure any excess water drains. Also, water below

---

17. Cunningham, *Cunningham's Encyclopedia of Magical Herbs*, 69.

18. Cunningham, *Cunningham's Encyclopedia of Magical Herbs*, 86.

the leaves, making sure not to get the stems or leaves damp, as this can lead to rot. Treat this plant as you would a cherished relationship, giving it attentive care.

Fern (**Polypodiopsida**)

Ferns are one of those plants that just look magickal; folklore is riddled with references to ferns. These plants have been found in fossil records dating back to the middle Devonian period 360 million years ago, meaning they are one of the most ancient plant species. And ferns as a species are found throughout the world in a variety of habitats. Ferns, specifically the Boston fern, have been noted by NASA as excellent air purifiers.[19]

According to Cunningham, ferns have magickal properties of protection, luck, riches, and health, while they symbolize health, love, and protection.[20]

Ferns need indirect and low light. They like high humidity, which you can give them by placing the potted plant on a pebble-filled saucer you keep filled with water. The water in the saucer will evaporate, giving the fern the humidity it needs. They need temperatures around 70 degrees Fahrenheit. Their soil should be kept damp (not soaking), so they should be watered a little bit every day. Because of these preferences, ferns make excellent plants to keep in bathrooms, as the low light, heat, and humidity will keep the plants happy and healthy.

19. Wolverton, Douglas, and Bounds, "A Study of Interior Landscape Plants for Indoor Air Pollution Abatement."

20. Cunningham, *Cunningham's Encyclopedia of Magical Herbs*, 115.

Golden Pothos (**Epipremnum aureum**)

This plant is probably the most ubiquitous houseplant found in office settings. It is an easy-to-maintain plant that grows rapidly and can be propagated practically effortlessly. One only has to cut a trailing piece of the plant under a root node and plop it in a glass of water. In just a few days, it will be sending out roots. I once had a golden pothos whose vines encircled my living room, supported by cup hooks driven into the ceiling. The heart-shaped leaves and bright green foliage can give an air of lush abundance to any space. It is also another one of NASA's air-cleaning plants.[21] *Note:* the plant is toxic, so keep it away from any animals or children who might be tempted to nibble on it.

Golden pothos is native to the Solomon Islands. Due to its fast-growing nature, it is easy to recognize its magickal properties of prosperity. As it is a hardy plant with heart-shaped leaves, it symbolizes perseverance and longing. A business prosperity spell involves writing down what you want (more revenue, increased customers, better sales, etc.) on a slip of paper, placing it in a pot of soil, and then planting a cutting of golden pothos in the pot. As the plant grows, so will your particular prosperity goal.

Golden pothos prefers bright indirect light. If the leaves start to pale, it means the plant is getting too much light. Let the soil dry out completely before watering. It will tell you when it needs to be watered; when the leaves start to droop, give it a drink. Overwatering will lead to root rot. It prefers a temperature between 65 and 75 degrees Fahrenheit and slight humidity. This is another plant that does well in bathrooms for the same reason as ferns.

---

21. Wolverton, Douglas, and Bounds, "A Study of Interior Landscape Plants for Indoor Air Pollution Abatement."

English Ivy (**Hedera helix**)

English ivy is one of those plants that is recognizable to even the least botanically minded individual. It also has a long history in folklore, religion, and magick, making it the perfect plant to have on hand to aid in spellwork. Like several other plants in this section, it has been noted by NASA as a proficient air purifier, specifically in its ability to remove mold from the air.[22]

English ivy is native to Europe. It is often paired with holly, another sacred and magickal plant, by Druids. The plant is sacred to Bacchus, who wears a crown of ivy and grape leaves. It has magickal properties of protection and healing. It symbolizes both peace and fidelity, and so ivy can be used in reconciliation spells to heal rifts between friends.

English ivy prefers low indirect light. It should be kept away from doors and windows or other places where there are drafts, as it prefers a steady temperature (either warm or cool, just as long as the temperature remains the same). It requires damp (not soaking) soil and should be watered regularly. Do not let the soil dry out. English ivy is often planted in hanging containers. Vines can be trimmed and propagated into new plants.

Jade Plant (**Crassula ovata**)

The jade plant has been my constant disappointment. I have never managed to keep one alive, despite the fact that it is one of those plants that is known to be easy to maintain. Perhaps it is my fiery Aries nature that just isn't compatible with the succulent. Or maybe it's because I've tried to grow it during times of serious financial hardship that the plants just couldn't thrive. Whatever the

---

22. Wolverton, Douglas, and Bounds, "A Study of Interior Landscape Plants for Indoor Air Pollution Abatement."

case, my failures should not dissuade you from bringing this plant into your home.

Jade plants originated in South Africa. It is used in feng shui for its properties of prosperity and success. Specifically, jade plants have magickal powers of financial success. This is another plant that is often grown in businesses to attract financial prosperity. Include the succulent in any money or job spells you might cast. The plant also symbolizes growth and renewal and can be used in rituals marking birthdays, anniversaries, and other milestones.

Jade plants prefer full sunlight for at least four hours a day. During spring and summer, they should be watered so that the soil is moist (not soaking). During fall and winter, let the soil dry out between waterings. As for temperature, jade plants respond well to higher temperatures (65 to 70 degrees Fahrenheit) in the summer and cooler temperatures (50 degrees Fahrenheit) in winter.

Jasmine (**Jasminum polyanthum**)

This is one of the few fragrant houseplants. The scent of jasmine has been shown in studies to reduce anxiety and improve sleep quality, making it a beneficial bedroom plant. Exposing the plant to cool temperatures in fall can encourage blooms in February, meaning you'll have flowers at the tail end of winter.

Jasmine is native to Eurasia, Australasia, and Oceania, although the plant usually cultivated as a houseplant is found in China and Burma (Myanmar). It has magickal properties of love, money, and prophetic dreams.[23] In plant language it symbolizes love, beauty, and sensuality. You can add jasmine flowers to dream pillows to encourage dreams, especially if the flowers come from a plant that you keep in your bedroom.

---

23. Cunningham, *Cunningham's Encyclopedia of Magical Herbs*, 147.

Jasmine likes bright light, with some limited direct light (a couple of hours a day). The plant likes moist (not wet) soil, especially when it is in bloom. You can place the plant outside during the summer and for a short period of time during the fall. Jasmine is a vine plant that will require support if you let it send out tendrils. Otherwise, prune to keep growth lateral.

Peace Lily (**Spathiphyllum wallisii**)

Yet another NASA-approved plant, the peace lily is a general air cleanser.[24] Despite its name, this is not a true lily. It does, however, share the similarity of being toxic to people and pets if ingested, so this is a plant to keep out of reach of any grazers, be they human or animal.

The peace lily is native to the tropical rainforests of Columbia and Venezuela. Its magickal properties are of comfort, harmony, calming energy, protection, and cleansing, especially with regard to spirits. As its name suggests it symbolizes peace, as well as sympathy. This plant is well-suited for spells to influence the end of wars or to encourage understanding and sympathy between conflicting parties. If you are bothered by unwanted spirits in your home, bring in a potted peace lily and place in the most affected area. Also, because the plant's growing needs make it an ideal bathroom plant, it can be useful for magic and rituals that involve self-love and acceptance.

Peace lilies need little light. If the leaves are yellowing, that means the plant is getting too much sunlight. When the leaves begin to droop, water it. During the summer, you can mist the leaves for an added bit of moisture. The plant can tolerate a wide

---

24. Wolverton, Douglas, and Bounds, "A Study of Interior Landscape Plants for Indoor Air Pollution Abatement."

range of temperatures (between 65 to 85 degrees Fahrenheit), but doesn't like cold (below 45 degrees Fahrenheit). Keep the plant away from doors and windows and drafts to keep it happy.

Snake Plant (**Sansevieria trifasciata**)

Snake plant is also known by the name of mother-in-law's tongue, Saint George's sword, bowstring hemp, and devil's tongue, all of which allude to the properties of this plant. The leaves are sword-like, indicating that it is a defensive plant. It is another plant noted by NASA as an air cleaner, although it is toxic to pets. [25]

Snake plant is native to West Africa. Its magickal properties are protective, specifically against any enemies and any hexes sent your way. Create a living protective talisman by painting protective eyes on the pot in which a snake plant is potted. Add crystals like smoky quartz, black tourmaline, or amethyst on top of the soil to amplify the protective energies. The plant symbolizes cleanliness and tenacity.

Snake plants require bright indirect light. Let the soil dry out between waterings and then water thoroughly. The soil should be wet but not soaking, as water-soaked roots will rot. It does well in average room temperature but should be kept from any drafts or cold spots.

Spider Plant (**Chlorophytum comosum**)

Spider plants are another low-maintenance plant that is an efficient air cleaner. They are often set in hanging planters to take advantage of their dramatic cascading effect. Like golden pothos, spider

---

25. Wolverton, Douglas, and Bounds, "A Study of Interior Landscape Plants for Indoor Air Pollution Abatement."

plants are easily propagated from the small "spiderettes" that dangle from the ends of the plant like spiders on a web.

Spider plants originated in South and West Africa. They are associated with the element of air. The plant has magickal properties of protection, fertility, and the ability to absorb negativity. Hang a plant in your kitchen window for prosperity. In the language of plants it symbolizes mindfulness and health, making this a good plant to have near your meditation space, if you have one such set aside.

Provide spider plants with bright indirect sunlight. Keep the soil moist (but not soggy), allowing it to dry out between waterings. The plant prefers slightly cooler temperatures (between 55 and 65 degrees Fahrenheit), making it tolerant of the parts of your home that are not as well heated as others.

Venus Flytrap (**Dionaea muscipula**)

Venus flytraps are possibly the strangest plants in this section. As carnivorous plants, they require a different level of care than the others. They require actual prey to survive, which means if you grow them, you'll need to provide them with the occasional fly to dine on. They also require distilled water. The minerals and salts found in tap or bottled water can kill them.

Venus flytraps originate in North and South Carolina in the United States. Like many plants, they have magickal properties of protection. Unlike the defensive protection of the snake plant, however, this protection is one that is aggressive and can even involve preemptive attacks. You can use Venus flytraps in spells meant to trap negativity and hexes sent your way. They symbolizes strength and courage.

Venus flytraps require good drainage and specialized soil; no general-purpose potting soil will do. Terrariums are a good habitat for the plant, giving it the humidity and heat it needs to thrive. Provide it with bright indirect light. You will also have to feed it a fly every month or two.

EXERCISE
Plant Bonding

By virtue of being indoors, houseplants don't enjoy the cleaning actions of rain and wind. This means they get dusty, which can interfere with photosynthesis. Using a soft cloth, wipe down the leaves of your plant. As you do so, take notice of the plant. Are there any spots or browning? Are the leaves limp? Open yourself to the plant's energies. Do you sense anything? Is it trying to communicate to you? Do this exercise monthly as a way to form a bond with your plant allies.

Crafts

Incense Blends

Burning incense is one of the most common ways not only to connect with the element of air but also to release the magickal properties of herbs and plants.

Use	Blend	Ingredients
For when you need honest and clear communication	Clear Communication	• Allspice • Cinnamon • Nutmeg • Cloves
For when you need to get the creative juices flowing	Creative Thinking	• Lilac • Vervain • Horehound
For when things have gotten a bit tense	Peace and Harmony	• Meadowsweet • Lavender • Passionflower

Living Room Herbs

The following herbs are suited for magick dealing with the living room.

Allspice has magickal properties of harmony and sympathy. It increases cooperation between people. Use it when you have people over for entertaining to enhance people's enjoyment.

Carnations, lilacs, violets, nasturtium, and evening primrose all are flowers that are associated with creativity. Fill a vase with blooms of the same flower, or mix in several different types in a bouquet.

Meadowsweet is a good, all-purpose living room herb. It has associations with the air element and magickal properties to instill peace and harmony, friendship, and happiness.

Walnuts and almonds both foster mental clarity. Keep a bowl of walnuts in the shell (don't forget the nutcracker) or a can of almonds in the living room. Eat them whenever you need to clear your thoughts or sharpen your mind.

Wintergreen repels disharmony and promotes tranquility and peace in the home. Keep wintergreen mints or gum on hand for those who live in or visit your home to keep their words harmonious and positive.

Spells

Overcoming Artistic Blocks Talisman

This talisman can be used for any creative block, whether you are a writer working on your novel, are an artist working at the easel, or just need to come up with a thesis statement for your homework. The talisman requires 3 pieces of wood. They don't have to be very large, 3 inches or so long. Twigs are ideal. If you can, gather the wood during the waxing moon to draw inspiration and ideas to you. You will also need 1 piece of yellow ribbon or string 21 inches long.

Gather together a piece of pine (for mental clarity), a piece of mistletoe (for creativity), and a piece of beech (for inspiration). Tie the bundle together with the yellow ribbon, leaving enough to allow you to hang the talisman. As you tie the ribbon, say (aloud or in your head), "On the eastern wind, ideas come to me."

Hang your talisman from the ceiling over where you create. Allow the ends of the ribbon to dangle. When you feel the stale breath of a creative block at the back of your neck, focus on the talisman and draw down the properties of the woods into you. Keep the talisman free of dust.

Rituals

Start with the Breath

Aine Llewellyn, in her blog post "Breath, the Foundational Practice," suggests focusing on your breath for a few moments, at different times throughout the day. "Simply notice your breath. You don't need to change it—though you will inevitably end up breathing differently through the act of taking note. Focus on your breath for a few moments. Let yourself reconnect with your body. ... You may find yourself sinking into your feet and centering your body, naturally. Return to whatever you were doing, more grounded than before." [26]

This is similar to the practices of centering or grounding that I discuss in "Four Magickal Techniques" on page 27. It is like a pocket-size version of them. It brings the focus back onto you—how you breathe—and it helps to build the mental muscles and attention span needed for longer periods of meditation or centering. It also provides you with various times a day to pause and take stock of how you are doing. These brief rests interrupt the constant urge to *Go! Go! Go!* that our society instills in us. Interrupting that pace, sticking our heads up to assess our situation, keeps us from crashing, either from burnout or because we were so focused we didn't see the obstacles in front of us.

To get into the habit of performing this check-in, you might try to integrate it first into one of your daily chores or rituals. When you are doing the dishes or brushing your teeth, you might pause, focus on your breathing for five to seven breaths, and then go back to what you were doing. Or try it before you enter a room or situation to collect yourself. The added benefit of doing this regularly is that you will become used to taking that moment, stopping, and thinking before you act, which can help in situations where you want to make sure you are fully present, such as reading a tarot spread or in the middle of a spell.

---

26. Aine Llewellyn, "Breath, the Foundational Practice," *Patheos* (blog), January 24, 2020, https://www.patheos.com/blogs/ainellewellyn/2020/01/b-for-breath/.

Clear the Room

Traditionally, smoke is used to cleanse a space. If you are someone who suffers from respiratory issues, however, smoke cleansing might not be an option. Additionally, when dealing with spaces that include furniture, especially chairs and couches, there will be energies (and odors) trapped and stored in the fabric. With this in mind, the following ritual uses a room/fabric spray you are going to make ahead of time and have on hand for the after-visitor cleanup.

Room/Fabric Spray

You will need:

> 4-ounce spray bottle
>
> Rosemary essential oil
>
> Thyme essential oil
>
> Lemon essential oil
>
> Witch hazel or vodka
>
> Distilled water

Add 10 drops each of the rosemary, thyme, and lemon essential oils to the bottle. To that add 2 ounces of the witch hazel or vodka. Finally, add the distilled water.

Rosemary and thyme are herbs that have been used for millennia to cleanse space and make it sacred. Lemon has purification and cleansing properties that remove negativity. The three herbs work together to "reset" the energies of your space.

You will need to shake the bottle each time before you use it to make sure the ingredients are all mixed together.

The Cleansing

Before you cleanse the room, set it back to rights. If there are dishes, take them to the kitchen. Move furniture back to where it belongs. Put away anything that is out of place. Vacuum or sweep if necessary. Once the place is physically clean, it's time to work on the spiritual and magickal planes of the space.

To cleanse the room start at the east of the room. Spritz the air and say, "I reclaim my space." Visualize the spray spreading out into the air, breaking up and dispersing the energies, thought patterns, and magick left behind by your visitors. You can view the spray as a yellow ray cutting through the light gray of those leftover energies. Move to the north of the room, spritz the air, and say, "I reclaim my space." Continue moving in a counterclockwise direction around the room. Spray not only the air but any fabric furniture, pillows, throws, or any other fabric that might have absorbed the energy and odors of your guests. By the time you have reached your starting point, the whole room should feel lighter and clear.

7

THE BEDROOM:
PROSPERITY AND SLEEP

Bedrooms are a relatively recent development in architecture. With the exception of the rich, most people shared beds with their children, and those beds might not even be in a separate room. People came up with all sorts of ways to gain some privacy when it came to sleep, from the four-poster beds with their drapes to the closet-beds of the Netherlands. In modern times and in Western communities there is an expectation that people will have their own bedrooms, at the very least parents in one and the children in another. The bedroom has come to be regarded as a sanctuary, a place one can go to shut out the world.

The bedroom holds in it the energy of rest and restoration. This isn't the more dramatic and permanent rest of north and earth, when the deceased are returned to the ground to be reborn, and the cycle begins again. This is the small rest, the setting of the sun that signals the day is done and we should retreat to the safety of blankets and pillows. Tomorrow a new day will dawn, but now is the time to recover.

It is from the earth that all forms of abundance come. The metals that form our currency, the materials we use to build our factories and schools and homes, the oil that powers our cars, the food that fills our bellies—it all comes from the earth. And so when we rest, we are connecting to that wealth. When we ground, we tap into all the resources the earth has to offer. And when we dream, we live out our desires of riches and adventure and fulfillment, or we have nightmares about scarcity and deprivation.

Here in the bedroom our base need for security and our want for prosperity come together.

Crafts

Wire-Wrapped Crystal Pendant

Follow the instructions to create a quick and easy pendant from a crystal that you can then hang where you want its influence: on your headboard, the lamp next to your bed, in your window. For the wire, you can strip the paper or plastic from two twist ties. Keep your crystal pendant dusted. Charge it from time to time by letting it set out where the light from the full moon can touch it.

You will need:

> 2 pieces of wire 4 inches in length
>
> Crystal or stone 1 inch or less in circumference

1. Lay one wire atop the other like an equilateral cross.
2. Twist the bottom wire around the top wire. Then twist the top wire around the bottom one to form a knot.
3. Place the crystal on top of the wires, centered over the knot.
4. Bring two opposing wires up and over the crystal and twist them together.

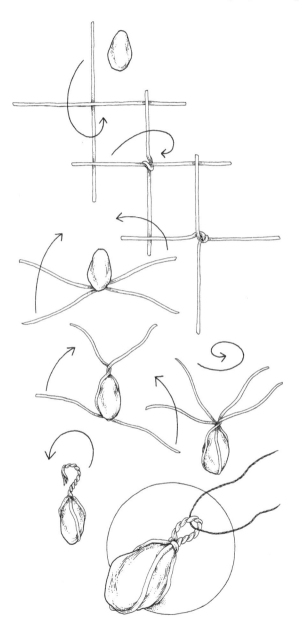

5. Bring the remaining two wires up and twist them onto the other wires.

6. Twist all four wires together and then bend them over to form a loop.

7. String a chain or length of cord through the top loop.

Bedroom Crystals

When using crystals or stones to aid in sleep, keep in mind that placement can be just as important as what crystal you use. Crystals under the pillow affect dreams. Under the bed they affect sleep. On the nightstand they affect the energies of the room. As the bedroom is a place of rest, you don't choose crystals that are too energetic. Always cleanse crystals before using them. Give them a sun or moon bath or smoke cleanse them.

Amethyst

Amethyst is an all-purpose sleep crystal. Its color links it to the mind. Magically, it helps with sleep and dreaming. It also has protective properties, warding off nightmares. Cunningham suggests placing amethyst under one's pillow to ensure a peaceful night's rest.[27] Practically, amethyst is a widely available stone. Beyond the tumbled stones one can find nearly everywhere, amethyst is fashioned into various species of jewelry and household goods, making it incredibly easy to incorporate this crystal into your bedroom sanctuary. You could hang an amethyst point from your headboard, keep an amethyst candleholder on your nightstand, or place an amethyst geode on your dresser.

---

27. Scott Cunningham, *Cunningham's Encyclopedia of Crystal, Gem, and Metal Magic* (St. Paul, MN: Llewellyn Publications, 2002), 72.

Lepidolite

Lepidolite is an anti-nightmare stone. It ranges in color from lilac to rose, indicating it is a gentler stone than amethyst. Its protective energies are more soothing than confrontational. If your sleep troubles stem from nightmares, this stone will protect you from them. Its connection to psychic powers makes it a good stone to use as protection when you are lucid dreaming or traveling in the astral plane or journeying. Use it in a talisman to hang on your headboard. Do not water cleanse this stone. It is good to use for anxiety.

Selenite

Selenite is named for Selene, a moon goddess, and has strong ties to the moon. It is a stone that promotes a peaceful atmosphere. It is protective, not only dispelling negative energy, but also providing a shield from negativity. This stone is useful in helping create a tranquil, restful space in your bedroom. To get the most out of it, first cleanse the space, both physically and magickally. Once your room is a clean slate, so to speak, place pieces of selenite in each corner of the room to create a protective grid. As you place them, visualize the shimmering, protective energy, like a bubble, enclosing the room, with the selenite being the anchor points. You can add more points—under and over your bed, for example—if you want.

This shield will need regular attention. Once a month or so, on the full moon, lie or sit on your bed. Close your eyes and reach out with your mind to the grid. Go over it, from point to point in all directions, looking for any weak points. As this is a bubble, make sure to check the bottom of it, where it encases the floor. If the shield feels weak, lay out the selenite to charge in the moon. At least twice a year you'll want to charge all the selenite as well.

Moonstone

Moonstone is another stone with strong ties to the moon (as the name suggests). It comes in the colors blue, pink, or white. Because of its magickal properties tied to divination, psychic powers, and sleep, this is the stone you want to use for prophetic dreams, lucid dreaming, and any travels you might take when asleep. Moonstone is another easily obtained stone due to its popularity. It can be found in jewelry, as beads, and tumbled stones. As this stone has a specific purpose—fostering prophetic dreams and protection when engaging in psychic activities—rather than a general purpose, it's best to store it away when not using it. Like the lepidolite, you could make a talisman by stringing five moonstone beads onto a blue ribbon and hanging them on your headboard.

Sleep Potion

I add this tincture to my nightly mug of tea. The soothing, sleepy qualities of the herbs help my body get ready for bed. I've given the potion to my children when they have a hard time sleeping, but I mix it with ¼ cup of water.

You will need:

> 3 tablespoons catnip
>
> 4 tablespoons chamomile flowers
>
> 3 tablespoons lavender blossoms
>
> 1 teaspoon licorice root
>
> Vodka

Place the herbs in a jar and cover with vodka. Place the jar in a dark place for 2 weeks. Shake the jar every 2 days. Strain out the herbs and store the tincture in a dropper jar.

To use, add 10 to 20 drops for adults (or 5 to 10 for children) to ¼ cup water and drink.

Jasmine Bedtime Spray

The scent of jasmine can lower anxiety, helping ease you to sleep. Once you have fallen asleep, you will have better and longer rest. The scent has been shown to lessen restless sleeping, giving you more hours of sleep.

You can keep a jasmine plant in your bedroom, but also take advantage of the essential oil to make a spray you can use on your pillow and blankets.

You will need:

> 1 ounce witch hazel
>
> 3 ounces distilled water
>
> Jasmine essential oil
>
> 4-ounce spray bottle

Add the witch hazel and water to the bottle. Then add 10 drops of the jasmine essential oil. Screw on the spray nozzle and shake the bottle to mix.

Hold the nozzle 10 inches away from your pillow and covers. Spritz them and wait about 30 seconds for the fabric to absorb the spray. Inhale the scent and let it carry you off to the land of Nod.

Jasmine also has the ability to induce prophetic dreams. If you are looking to dream about the future, you can use the spray just on your pillow before you bed down. Tell your dreaming mind what question you want answered as you fall asleep. When you wake up the next morning, write down what you dreamt about. The answers will be there.

Spells

Give a Penny, Take a Penny Spell

Money has energy that requires movement. If that movement is stymied, perhaps by huge sums being hoarded instead of circulated back into a community, you end up with a breakdown in the economy. This spell works on the concept that a rising tide lifts all boats. It is not meant to address the problems of wide-scale economic inequality but those on a smaller scale. Use this spell when you need a small influx of cash.

You will need 3, 7, or 9 pennies.

Charm the pennies with the following: "Wealth to me, wealth to thee." As you do so, envision every penny imbued with rich, golden energy.

Once the pennies are charged, take them with you shopping. Leave them in give a penny, take a penny trays at stores. As the pennies are taken up and used by others, prosperity in the form of small amounts of unexpected cash will come to you.

Sleep Protection Jar Spell

Sometimes you need more than a piece of selenite under your pillow to protect you when you sleep. If you engage in astral projection or lucid dreaming or often have nightmares, it might be time to break out some more involved spellwork. You will be creating a jar spell that will contain various materia magica with protective properties. By layering them one atop each other, you are amplifying your intent. Using a glass jar contains the spell within an object of earth, concentrating the magick. You can paint the outside of the jar in dark shades of blue and add protective symbols before you add the materials.

You will need:

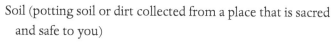

Soil (potting soil or dirt collected from a place that is sacred
and safe to you)

Small pieces of untumbled amethyst

Sea salt

Small jar with a lid

Gather your materials. Center and ground yourself. Add the
soil to the jar. Say (aloud or in your head), "The earth protects
me." Visualize being cradled in the comforting embrace of the
earth. Add the amethyst to the jar. Say (aloud or in your head),
"Nothing can harm me." Visualize any nightmares or any harmful entities getting caught up on the rough edges of the amethyst
and being unable to reach you. Pour in the sea salt. Say (aloud or
in your head), "Wherever I travel, I am safe." Visualize the white,
protective energy surrounding you when you sleep, so that even if
you leave your body, your astral form is shielded.

Seal the jar and place it under your bed. Every full moon, pull
it out and recharge it with your personal energy to continue its
protection. If you ever find you have to dismantle the jar, bury the
earth and salt. Cleanse the amethyst before you use it for any other
purpose.

Spell for Securing Your Prosperity

I struggled financially for a decade after I got divorced. It has only
been in the last year that I have finally gotten my feet under me. All
those years of hardship have instilled in me the need to protect this
newfound prosperity. If you find yourself in a similar situation, or
if you just want to safeguard what you already have, cast this spell.

Malachite's color ties it to monetary wealth (at least in the
United States, where paper money is printed with green ink). It
is also a protective stone, keeping misfortune at bay. Both golden

pothos and jade plants have deep associations with money, making either the perfect choice as a plant guardian. Both are also easy to maintain.

You will need:

> Piece of malachite
>
> Golden pothos or jade plant
>
> Soil
>
> Planter with saucer

Take the malachite in your hand and think about all that you have, your home, your job, your car, your money—whatever wealth you are trying to protect. Pour these thoughts into the malachite. This now represents your prosperity.

Add some soil to the planter. When it is about halfway filled, nestle the malachite in the soil. Say aloud or in your mind, "Earth, source of all wealth and abundance, keep my prosperity safe." Now plant the golden pothos or jade plant in the planter. Tell the plant, "Pothos/Jade, guard well my prosperity with your roots."

As the plant guardian keeps your wealth safe, you must tend to its needs: water, light, fertilizer. Keep the plant in your bedroom. If ever you are required to repot the plant, repeat the spell. If ever the plant dies, that is a sign your prosperity is in danger and you need to take measures to manage the problem.

Rituals

Create a Bedtime Routine

You'd think that sleep would be one of those activities everyone is good at. Just lie down, close your eyes, and go to sleep. However, the CDC found in 2016 that a third of adults in the United States aren't getting enough sleep, with insomnia being the most com-

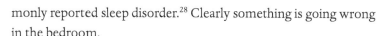

monly reported sleep disorder.[28] Clearly something is going wrong in the bedroom.

Some sleep disorders, like sleep apnea, require the treatment of a physician. I'm not going to address those as I am not a doctor (nor do I play one on TV). If you have trouble sleeping, you should get checked out, if you can. If you have trouble falling asleep at night, create a bedtime ritual.

Create a bedtime routine. By doing so, you are training your body and mind to switch over to sleep mode. A bedtime ritual or routine is very personal and has to take into account the vagaries of your life. However, there are some guidelines you can follow to create your own.

Read over the following and then sit down with paper and pencil to draft your own ritual. Do this during the day, at a time when you won't feel rushed. Don't do it when you are getting ready for bed. Treat it like you would writing a full moon or sabbat ritual. Give it care and detail, but also acknowledge that this first draft might need adjustment as you put it into actual practice. As you engage in your bedtime ritual, note what feels right or wrong. Does the order need to be changed up? Did you not give yourself enough time?

First, determine your "lights out" time. This is when you want to actually go to sleep. You are going to start your bedtime ritual forty-five minutes to an hour before that time. Ban all electronics when it's time to start your ritual: no phone, laptop, or game device in bed. The light from the screens has been shown to interfere with melatonin production, disrupting the sleep/wake cycle.

28. Yong Lui, Anne G. Wheaton, Daniel P. Chapman, Timothy J. Cunningham, Hua Lu, and Janet B. Croft, "Prevalence of Healthy Sleep Duration among Adults—United States, 2014," *Morbidity and Mortality Weekly Report* 65, no. 6 (February 19, 2016): 137–41, http://dx.doi.org/10.15585/mmwr.mm6506a1.

Choose instead to read a book, journal, make your to-do list for the next day, solve a word puzzle, or do another activity that doesn't involve a computer screen.

Play soft, relaxing music and dim the lights to create an atmosphere of rest and relaxation. You might even do something to signal you are going to sleep: blow out a candle, say goodnight to the universe, offer up a prayer, touch the crystal next to your bed. Whatever you choose, do it consistently so that you associate bedtime with that action.

If you work on this every night, in about two weeks' time, if not sooner, you should have a bedtime ritual that fits 99 percent of your actual lived life. And as your circumstances change, make sure to update the ritual as necessary.

Body Scan Relaxation Method

If you find yourself struggling to get to sleep because of racing thoughts or anxiety, try the following relaxation technique. By going through the different parts of your body, you give your mind something to focus on.

1. Lie in bed with your eyes closed. Uncross any limbs.

2. Start at the top of your head. Name each part of your body and tell it to relax. "Scalp, relax. Forehead, relax. Cheeks, relax." Don't try to force it; just bring your attention to the body part and tell it to relax.

3. Repeat "(Body part), relax" however many times you need before moving on to the next part. Get as detailed as you want, or just stick with the major body parts.

4. As you work down your body, feel it growing heavy and warm. You may feel yourself sinking into the bed.

5. If you reach your toes and are still awake, start again, this time working your way up your body to your head.

6. If intrusive thoughts try to get in the way, acknowledge the thought and tell it now is not the time and that you will address it tomorrow. Then return to the exercise.

Morning Ritual

We often treat waking up as if it is flipping a switch: one second we're asleep, the next we are awake. But the process is more like turning a dial. We awaken through stages. To help ease the transition from slumber to wakefulness, take a few moments to stretch. You don't even have to get out of bed. Reach your arms over your head and wiggle your fingers. Stretch out your legs and wriggle your toes. Sit up and twist from one side to the other to stretch out your back. Rotate your wrists and ankles. Roll your head and neck and shoulders.

You just spent several hours away from your body mentally, if not also metaphysically. Use this time to come back to your body fully and get the circulation moving. When you do roll out of bed, continue stretching, reaching for the sky and then down to your feet. Swing your arms and raise your knees. This is another kind of grounding and centering. You are using the movement of your body to shake off any remaining holds your dreams might have on you.

When you are feeling settled in your skin, greet the day. Say good morning to Hestia. Pull the blankets up over your bed and head out to start the day.

8
THE BATHROOM:
PURIFICATION AND HEALTH

The bathroom is associated with the water element. Emotions run close to the surface here: our insecurities over our appearance, our vulnerabilities, our beauty routines and health regimens. It's home to our medicine cabinet, our soaps and toothpaste, our creams and serums, all meant to keep us healthy. It is where we wash up, go to the toilet, puke, shave, and contemplate our navels on occasion.

Of all the rooms, the bathroom is the one where we can truly be alone. It can be a refuge and escape and a place of momentary relief, as any mother needing five minutes of alone time or any employee needing a break from their job can attest. The spells and rituals in this section are mostly centered on you: your health, your purification, your beauty. Self-care means more than facial masks and bubble baths. It includes making sure you are taking your medications and vitamins and cleansing both your physical and metaphysical bodies.

Your body is your temple. You can decorate, refurbish, and renovate it as you see fit. It is the only body you get in this lifetime, and so the sooner you embrace it—with all its quirks and unique architecture—the happier you'll be. In her refusal to marry and making Zeus recognize her right to body autonomy, Hestia supports abortion rights, sex worker rights, and LGBTQI rights, as well as aromantic and asexual rights. Her lessons include loving yourself and allowing every individual to feel comfortable in their own skin.

Crafts

Rosewater

Roses have been associated with love and beauty throughout history. Magickally, roses have properties of love, protection, and healing. The scent of roses is a mood booster, and rose petals have been used in various beauty products, specifically rosewater. When making this, use organic rose petals to avoid chemicals like pesticides getting into your rosewater.

Rosewater Recipe

You will need:

> Organic rose petals
>
> Water

Make rosewater just as you would distilled water. In a large pot place a bowl. Place the rose petals around the bowl in the pot. Then add just enough water to cover the rose petals.

Bring the water to a simmer and cover, with the lid upside down. Place ice in the lid. Let the pot simmer for 20 to 30 minutes. As with making the distilled water on page 53, replace the ice as it melts, using a turkey baster to remove the water if you want.

Remove the water from the bowl and store in a glass container that closes tightly. Store in the fridge for 3 to 4 months.

Use rosewater in various love spells. Add an ounce to your cleaning water to add more loving energies to your home. Add an ounce to your laundry water before going on a date. Add to room sprays.

You can make floral waters using other flowers and herbs as well.

Rosewater Toner

You will need:

> 1 tablespoon rosewater
>
> 4 tablespoons distilled water
>
> 2½-ounce spray bottle

Combine rosewater and distilled water in the spray bottle. Shake to mix. Mist on dry skin to hydrate it. Spray it on a cotton ball and wipe over your face after cleansing to soothe the skin.

Sugar Scrubs

In 2017 the United States banned soaps and body washes that contained microbeads—tiny plastic particles meant to provide exfoliation. Unsurprisingly, the microbeads turned out to be an environmental hazard. Sugar scrubs provide soft, moisturized skin without such problems. It also offers you the ability to fine-tune beauty products to your own specific needs.

You can add any oil to the sugar scrub; you just want to keep the ratio of 4 parts sugar to 1 part oil. Sugar is used because it is gentle on skin, readily available, and cheap. Play around with different essential oils to find scents and combinations that you like.

The scrub should only be used once or twice a week. Take the opportunity to use it as a thorough body cleanser, stripping away any buildup of negativity, the expectations of others, any psychic detritus, or anything else that is unhealthy and clinging to you just as it scrubs away dead skin. This regular cleansing is just as important to your well-being as all other regular hygiene routines.

Sugar scrubs, if stored properly in a tightly sealed airtight container, keep for up to one month in the refrigerator, meaning you can make up a batch ahead of time, to tap into various astrological timing.

You will need:

> 4 tablespoons white sugar
>
> 1 tablespoons coconut oil
>
> A couple of drops of peppermint essential oil

Mix up the ingredients in a bowl just before you shower. Take the bowl into the shower with you, keeping it away from the water. After washing, use your hands to scoop the sugar and scrub your skin with it. Rinse yourself clean.

Shower Purification Tabs

Traditionally, ritual baths are taken to purify and cleanse the body before rituals or spellwork. Baths aren't always practical, or you might not have time for one. Showers can provide the same purifying action. The shower tabs below use the purification properties of both lemon and rosemary to enhance the process. Place one or two on the floor of the tub or shower away from the bulk of the spray. As droplets of water land on the tabs, they will fizz, releasing the scent of the essential oils. The recipe below makes approximately 15 shower tabs.

You will need:

> 1 cup baking soda
>
> ½ cup cream of tartar
>
> 15 drops of lemon essential oil
>
> 15 drops of rosemary essential oil
>
> ¼ cup witch hazel
>
> Wax paper and a baking sheet, or a silicone ice cube mold

1. Mix the baking soda and cream of tartar together in a bowl.
2. Add the essential oils drop by drop, stirring between each drop.
3. Add witch hazel a teaspoon at a time, stirring between teaspoons, until the mixture clumps and holds its shape when you squeeze it in your hand. Work carefully so as not to activate the baking soda. You may not need to use all the witch hazel.

4. Line a baking sheet with wax paper. Fill a tablespoon with the mixture, packing it down tightly. Upend the tablespoon onto the wax paper. The shower tab mixture should slide out of the tablespoon with no trouble, but you can give it a firm tap if you need. Repeat until you have used up all the mixture. Alternatively, you can pack the mixture into silicone ice cube molds. Leave the mixture to dry overnight.

5. Once dry, remove the tabs from wax paper or pop them out of the mold, and store them in an airtight container.

Herbal Remedies

The herbal remedies that I write about below are not meant to be a replacement for medical attention. As a witch I believe in magick, but I also know that science works. I don't see the two in conflict but as working in conjunction with one another, which is why I get my flu shot every year but also make sure I have plenty of citrus honey tea on hand during cold and flu season.

Healing Teas

I am a proponent for using teas in remedies because they are simple, don't require hard-to-get materials, and are versatile. You can drink them, bathe in them, steam them, and even make syrups. Sip mint teas to help with your digestion or ginger tea to settle an upset stomach.

Thyme Tea

Use this tea for when you have a cough. Thyme is an expectorant, helping loosen up mucus so it is easier to cough up. It also is an antispasmodic, preventing and relieving spasms (i.e., coughing).

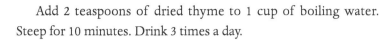

Add 2 teaspoons of dried thyme to 1 cup of boiling water. Steep for 10 minutes. Drink 3 times a day.

Citrus Cold Remedy Tea

Every cold and flu season I keep this tea on hand. The lemons provide a dose of vitamin C to help boost the immune system. The ginger helps ease coughing. Raw honey is antimicrobial and soothes sore throats.

You will need:

> 2 lemons thinly sliced, with peel
>
> 2 inches ginger root, peeled and mashed
>
> 1 cup raw honey

Mix all the ingredients together. Store in an airtight jar in the refrigerator for up to 1 month. To use, add 1 heaping tablespoon of the tea to a cup and add 1 cup of boiling water.

Hot Toddy

My husband swears by this as his go-to for when he's feeling run down, and I've honestly seen him rally after spending a day sipping them. The benefits of honey and lemon have been covered in previous recipes. Whiskey was dubbed the "water of life" by Irish monks in the Middle Ages. If you feel a cold coming on, make yourself a mug and settle in for an early night.

You will need:

> 1 shot of whiskey
>
> 1 tablespoon honey
>
> Squeeze of lemon
>
> 8 ounces hot water

In a mug add the whiskey, honey, and lemon. Pour in boiling water, stir, and drink.

Bath Salts

You can make bath salts up ahead of time for later use. For salts meant to ease sore muscles or cold symptoms, prepare them during the waning moon to tap into its banishing properties. To make the recipes below, mix all ingredients together and store in an airtight container. Add ¼ cup of salts to your bath while the water is running to dissolve the salts. Soak at least 20 minutes to get the full benefits of them.

Sore Muscle Bath Salts

2 cups Epsom salts

1 cup baking soda

10 drops peppermint essential oil

5 drops eucalyptus essential oil

5 drops rosemary essential oil

5 drops lavender essential oil

Congestion Bath Salts

1 cup Epsom salts

½ cup baking soda

5 drops peppermint essential oil

10 drops eucalyptus essential oil

Spells

Charms

I take medication for my depression and anxiety. I recognize that my mental health issues are based on the way my brain chemistry works and those medications help to address that. I also experience a metaphysical side of my illness. Artists will often depict these issues as spirits, demons, monsters, and so on that exist outside ourselves. Whether these mental illness entities are expressions of the disease or organisms drawn to those who have the mental illness is a topic for another time. The point here is that I will charm my medication to banish those metaphysical entities.

The same can be done with any medication. You can charm it to boost its effectiveness, to provide protection against the illness you are being treated for, to bolster your immune system, and more. If you take a medication before you sleep, you could charm it to help you fall asleep. Charm cough medicine to give you peace as you recover. There are any number of ways you can use charming to complement the healthcare you are already receiving. Keep in mind, however, this is an addition to your treatment and not meant to replace it.

Other Charming Ideas

- Charm your makeup for glamour or concealment.
- Charm your shoes so that you never lose your way or so that you never turn your ankle (as someone who is very clumsy, this is especially useful for me).
- Charm your soaps, body washes, and shampoos for purification to cleanse both your physical and metaphysical body.
- Charm your vitamins to strengthen your aura and personal protective shield.

- Charm your glasses and sunglasses to help you see through lies and illusions.

Spell to Banish the Jerk Brain

Call them brain weasels, gremlins, Jerk Brain, your enemy, or what have you, this spell targets the voice inside your head that tells you that you are weak, useless, and powerless or otherwise tries to get you to hate yourself. It can be hard to ignore its hateful whisperings, especially if you have lived with this voice for a long time.

The thing is, however, that this voice is just another entity, one that is haunting your mind rather than a battlefield. And as an entity, it can be targeted with magick.

You will need:

> Sheet of toilet paper
>
> Black pen
>
> Red pen
>
> Ground black pepper, cayenne pepper, red pepper, white pepper, or a combination of them
>
> Toilet
>
> 1 cup lemon rosemary water (see page 174)

On the sheet of toilet paper, with the black pen, draw a picture of your Jerk Brain, draw a symbol of it, or even just write down what you call it. Take care not to rip the paper. If you do, start over. As you work, visualize the voice being pulled into and trapped in the sheet.

Once you have trapped the Jerk Brain in the sheet, use the red pen to draw a circle around the representation. As you do so say, "You are trapped. You can't escape." Again, it is important that the sheet doesn't tear.

Sprinkle the pepper over the sheet, making sure to cover every part of the representation. Then gather up the corners and edges of the paper, keeping the pepper from falling out. Wad the paper into a ball in your fist. Envision your Jerk Brain, trapped in that paper, crushed. Say, "You are buried, you are crushed."

Drop the wad into the toilet and flush it. Say, "You are flushed, you are banished." Envision the wad of paper, pepper, and your Jerk Brain being carried away to the sewer.

Follow up by pouring the lemon rosemary water into the toilet and flushing it. This helps purify and protect that point of access into your home, ensuring that your Jerk Brain can't return through it.

Rituals

Love Eyes

Sometimes I do a thing. I call it looking at people with love eyes. I don't know if that is a term I heard somewhere or not. It involves consciously looking at others with the most positive thoughts I can come up with.

The woman who took a speed table a little too fast? I see her and think, "I've done that too, lady. It happens to all of us. I hope wherever you and your kids are going is awesome."

The man eating his fast food at the stop light? "I've been there, buddy. I hope your food is delicious and doesn't spill all over you."

I deliberately try to see the physical beauty in strangers. I try to find some mannerism or article of clothing or facial expression that I can connect with. I look for physical beauty because I don't know the people in order to assess their inner qualities. And by focusing on the physical and seeing it as beautiful, I expand my definition of what is beautiful beyond the narrow definitions beauty magazines, television, and films insist on.

I do this most often when things aren't going well for me. I do it because I have an inborn distrust, even dislike, of people. If I don't try to connect, I run the risk of falling into a mindset of seeing everyone I don't personally know as just bodies that take up space and get in the way.

This isn't a ritual to fix things, but a way for me to connect to humanity rather than being angry at how messed up the world can seem at times. Practice this ritual when you feel overwhelmed with frustration or sadness. All you need do is go out into the world, and sit somewhere you can observe people. Then watch them with love eyes. You can view them as you would through a social media filter with soft pink light and hearts around them, if that helps. Watch them without judgment. Keep at it for at least ten minutes, then go back to what you were doing.

Purification

It is no coincidence that the first advice given at the start of the COVID-19 pandemic involved hand washing. We were instructed to soap thoroughly, to wash vigorously, and to scrub for long enough for it to be effective. Social media was awash in memes about the different songs you could sing to ensure you were washing your hands for the right amount of time.

Washing has been a method of purification forever. Water cleanses us, taking away not only the dirt but also those baneful energies that might cling to our metaphysical bodies. And yet it is easy to overlook the simplicity of washing our hands when faced with the other options we have for purification. Perhaps now is the time to return to just water and soap and our hands.

You can incorporate herbal magickal properties into your purification washing by using soaps with ingredients like mint, citrus, or lavender essential oils or coconut oil. You can also add five or so drops of those essential oils to your soap to imbue it with those properties. When you lather your hands, not only be mindful of the physical act of washing, but visualize the suds breaking up clinging energies so that they can be shed as well.

Rinse your hands clean, visualizing the dirt and negativity being carried away down the drain. Dry your hands thoroughly with a clean towel.

Self-Love Ritual

The musician Lizzo said during her 2019 NPR Tiny Desk concert, "I just want everyone to remember: if you can love me, you can love yourself. Every single day. If you can love my big black ass at this tiny, tiny little desk, you can love yourself."[29] This call for self-love is one that is hard for many people to hear. We are inundated every day with advertisements and media telling us that we are not good enough in our bodies as they are. Pills, exercise, and surgery are all marketed to us as necessary for having a form that is worth love.

The ritual below is for combatting that incessant chatter—which only cares about separating you from your money and nothing else. You will need a lotion that you love: you love how it smells, you love how it makes your skin feel, you love how it feels when you use it.

Set up the bathroom to make it soft, supportive, and romantic even. Light candles, put on music that makes you feel good. Make sure the temperature is just right. Cover any mirrors. The point of this ritual is to engage with your body as it is, not with a reflection of it that might cause you to judge it.

---

29. Lizzo, "Tiny Desk Concert," *NPR* video, 16:59, July 29, 2019, min. 15:55–16:11, https://www.npr.org/2019/07/29/732097345/lizzo-tiny-desk-concert.

Remove all your clothes. Hold the lotion container in your hand and breathe love into it. See soft pink light flowing out from your hands into the bottle and infusing the lotion it contains. Continue until you can feel love emanating from the bottle. Now use the lotion on every part of your body.

As you rub it into your skin, think about all the important aspects of your body: how it moves you from one place to another, the ways that it is strong and capable, the ways that it is vulnerable and weak. Thank your body for all it does for you. Tell it you love it just as it is. Ask your body what it needs from you. Really listen to what it has to say.

Look at anything that might be labeled a "defect" or "imperfect" by society—wrinkles, liver spots, stretch marks, fat rolls, or flabby skin—see them as part of you, as testaments to the life you have lived. Be kind to your body and yourself, and know that you are beautiful and worthy of love. Love yourself, even if only for the moments that you are engaged in this ritual. When you are done, you can dress and go about your day.

Repeat this ritual often, at least once a season.

Drink to Your Health Ritual

The simplest of rituals involves only a glass of water. There's some back and forth over how much water a person is supposed to drink in a given day, but there is a general consensus that hydration is important. This ritual not only serves to help you quench your thirst but reminds you to give your body what it needs.

Pour a glass of water. It doesn't matter what kind. Ordinary tap water is often just as good as fancy filtered water. Hold the glass in your hands and say (aloud or in your head), "Hestia, grant me health." Visualize the water infused with white, healing light.

Drink the water down. As you drink, visualize the light suffusing your body. The water is carrying that healing to every cell, to every organ of your body. By the time you have finished the glass, your whole body should be glowing, if only for a brief moment.

You can add ingredients to your water, a wedge of lemon or slices of cucumber, if you wish. They aren't necessary, but if they help make the water more palatable to you, they're welcome additions. Perform this ritual at least once a day, morning, noon, or night—the timing doesn't matter.

9

BREAKING BREAD:
FEEDING YOUR BODY AND SPIRIT

Once upon a time families setting up a new household had access to several sources of wisdom and advice on what was needed and expected. In the late 1800s *Mrs. Beeton's Book of Household Management* was a best-selling title, along with other housekeeping manuals, that gave instruction on how to maintain a household. Over the past few generations the instruction on household matters fell to home economics courses. But in even more recent years, those classes have often been cut from school curriculums due to budget shortfalls, the result being that people are being expected to make a home when they have no idea where to start.

This chapter and the next are meant to deal with that gap in knowledge. They're not meant to be the be-all and end-all of housekeeping but a starting point. And they're written from the perspective of including spellwork and Hestia in homemaking. This chapter covers cooking and eating. I am keeping a lot of the advice general. Household manuals of the past were sought out because people wanted to conform their lives to a particular ideal. I'm of the mind that it is better for people to adapt ideals to their particular lives. The first section deals with kitchenware and how to take care of it. The second part covers recipes.

Food can be a tricky topic for some. Disordered eating, food insecurity, and other concerns can distort our relationship with food. If you are dealing with issues, be gentle with yourself as you read through this chapter. At its most simple, food is fuel for our bodies. We need calories and nutrients in order to survive. Taste, texture, and presentation are all incidental to this. And yet, humans have created all sorts of traditions and rituals surrounding food. Eating has been a communal activity for years. Even in today's age of workaholism, where people will eat lunch at their desks (or skip meals altogether to keep working), we have an impulse to share meals with others. The trend of posting pictures of one's meals to social media is an expression of that desire.

Kitchenware

There is a dizzying number of kitchen devices and tools available, making it seem that one has to have every gadget in order to prepare food. The reality is, though, most specialized tools are only going to be used by a small number of cooks. If you don't have a need for a bread maker or a strawberry huller, why would you buy one? I'm not advocating minimalism in the sense that you should have only one pot, one spoon, and one knife, but the items you have in your kitchen should be tools you use, else they just take up space and add an aura of wasted potential to the kitchen. I am also not against kitchen appliances. My slow cooker and rice cooker get heavy use from me. The aforementioned bread maker, however, wouldn't, as I would rather put the time and effort in baking bread in the oven. You, however, might not and might find the bread maker essential to having fresh bread on hand. The point is to make sure you are using all the items you keep in the kitchen.

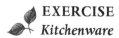

EXERCISE
Kitchenware

Pull out all your cooking implements, all the pots and pans, baking dishes, spoons, spatulas, can openers, knives, and countertop appliances. If it is used to cook with, it comes out for inspection. Arrange everything on your countertops and table.

Inspect everything and ask yourself the following questions:

1. What items have you used in the past year? In the past month?

2. What items are broken?

3. What items are worn out, rusted, cracked, and so on? Which knives have dull blades?

Sort everything into categories: tools you don't use, broken tools, tools that need to be replaced, and tools to keep.

Be honest with yourself about the tools you don't use. Look at the pots and pans. Do you use them often? Having the right size pot makes the difference in cooking, so if you only use the ginormous soup pot only to heat up canned soup, you might be better off with a smaller sauce pot. Look to see that you have all the parts too: lids that fit and owner's manuals for appliances.

If you have a Bundt pan you use once a year to make a cake for a holiday, you will want to keep it. But do you really use it at least once a year? If not, you can safely let it go. Many libraries have started cooking collections, loaning out specialty baking pans. There's also the possibility of borrowing pans from friends. The point is to be sure the cooking tool is actually getting used, rather than sitting shoved at the back of the cupboard, or worse, confronting you every time you open the pantry for something else, guilting you for not using it.

Tools that are in good, working condition can be donated, given away, or sold. Those that are damaged or broken should be thrown out or recycled. You might even search the internet for ideas on how to reuse or upcycle them to avoid adding to landfills.

The remaining items should be kitchen tools that you use regularly and are in good order. Give your cupboards a thorough cleaning. Anoint your kitchen tools with your Hestia oil, saying, "Hestia, bless these tools that they may help me in making food that is good for my body, mind, and soul" or words to that effect. Return them to the cupboards.

Dishes

When I graduated from high school, I received several gifts. Three of them—a slow cooker, an electric kettle, and a set of plastic cooking spoons—ended up being the most useful and long lasting of the bunch. The slow cooker served me for almost twenty years, and I still use the electric kettle and the spoons.

Alternately, by my early thirties, I had in my possession three sets of dishes—each containing twelve place settings. I also had a sideboard that housed a great deal of crystal that had never left the box. All of it had come to me as hand-me-downs and gifts. For a family of three, this was ridiculous. I had stored these sets for years out of a sense of obligation. And every time I saw the various plates and bowls and mugs I felt guilty that I wasn't using them. That sort of emotional weight isn't something anyone should feel, especially with regard to anything dealing with eating. It took my divorce for me to feel permitted to let go of it all. In the wake of donating the stonewear, porcelain, and crystal, I bought four place settings in a design and material I liked. Without the excess dishes, I had no need for the sideboard (another hand-me-down from my former mother-in-law that never suited my style) and donated it as well, leaving me with more space, both physically and emotionally.

Hand-me-downs and gifts can be a great way to stock your kitchen when you are starting out. If these gifts aren't your style, aren't useful, or engender a feeling of obligation, you are better off passing them on as soon as you are able. Your home should house items that make you feel safe and comforted or items toward which you have neutral feelings at the very least.

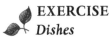

EXERCISE
Dishes

Pull out all your plates, bowls, glasses, cups, utensils, and anything else you eat off of, including any serving dishes. Arrange them on your table so you can see everything clearly.

Now consider your dishes:

1. Do you have enough, at least one place setting for everyone in your household? Do you have too many? Do you use each dish at least once in the week so that they all see equal usage rather than one plate being used over and over?

2. Do you like your dishes? Are the color and pattern pleasing to you? Do you like the material they're made of—do they feel good in your hands? Eating involves more than your sense of taste, and how your food is presented can enhance your enjoyment of the meal. So your dinnerware should help with that.

3. Are any of the dishes broken, chipped, or cracked? Are your knives dull and blunted when they should be sharp?

Sort your dishes accordingly: those that are broken and should be tossed; those you don't like or use to be donated, given away, or sold; and those you intend to keep.

Using your Hestia anointing oil, anoint each dish you mean to keep. Hold the dish upside down in your receiving hand. Dip the index finger of your dominant hand into the oil and then touch the dish. As you anoint it, say or think, "Hestia, bless this dish so that any food eaten from it may be nourishing and comforting," or words of that nature. Once you have blessed all your dishes (even the forks, spoons, and knives), give your cupboards and drawers a deep cleaning before putting the dishes back.

What if you only have dishes you aren't thrilled with and can't replace them? This is where you make peace with what you have to work with right now. Sit with the dishes and see, first, if there is anything you like about them. Try to think of that feature whenever you use them. If the dishes were a gift from someone you have a strained or less than friendly relationship with, cleanse them with smoke or water to remove as much of that person's energy from them. Try to view them in as neutral a light as possible. Instead of referring to them as "the dishes my toxic aunt gave me," view them as "the dishes that hold my delicious, nurturing food."

Taking Care of It All

Whether your dishes and kitchen tools are brand new or hand-me-down, you want to take proper care of them so they will last. Most dishes will need only washing and drying. Items like wooden spoons, stainless steel appliances, and cast-iron cookware require particular care.

Wood

No, this isn't something you eat, but a wood conditioner. It is made from two ingredients, both of which are nontoxic. Wooden utensils, bowls, and cutting boards should be hand washed and dried, but I will admit to tossing my wooden spoons into the dishwasher more often than not. My use of the spoon butter, however, helps them weather that rough treatment without cracking or splitting.

The recipe below makes enough to treat dozens of wooden utensils and dishes. Store it in an airtight container in your pantry.

You will need:

> 1 ounce beeswax
>
> 4 ounces coconut oil

1. Fill a saucepan with 2 cups of water. Place a smaller pan into the saucepan. Make sure the water does not get into the smaller pan.

2. Add the beeswax to the smaller pan and heat the water until it is just boiling. Melt the beeswax.

3. Add the coconut oil to the melted beeswax and stir until it has melted and the two have combined.

4. Remove the smaller pan from the heat. Carefully pour the melted wax and oil into a jar and let cool.

To use, take up a generous amount of the butter on a rag and rub on your wooden utensils, dishes, and cutting boards. The butter might be a bit hard when you start, but it will warm up and melt as you work with it. Let the wooden items sit overnight. The butter will soak in, leaving the wood smooth, conditioned, and dry, ready for use. Reapply as needed.

Cast Iron

A cast-iron skillet is one of those pieces of cookware I feel everyone should have. The fact that it can be used on the stovetop and oven means it can reduce the number of pans you use when cooking a meal. I've used my skillet to cook everything from bacon to eggs to pork chops to pilafs and even bread. Cast iron can be picked up from secondhand stores for cheap.

Keeping your cast iron in good working order is simply a matter of seasoning it, which really just means keeping it oiled. Seasoning the skillet is supposed to allow for nonstick cooking, but as I always use olive oil when I cook, I've never had need for that feature. For me, seasoning means easier clean up. To season your cast-iron skillet, do the following:

1. Wipe the inside of the skillet with olive oil. You want to coat the bottom and sides.

2. Preheat the oven to 350 degrees Fahrenheit

3. Place the skillet into the oven, upside down. You can put a baking sheet beneath it to catch any oil drips if you want.

4. Leave it in the oven for 1 hour. Afterward, turn off the heat and leave until the oven has cooled. Pull out the skillet, ready for use.

You will have to repeat the seasoning on occasion as the oil will start to come off, especially if you use soap to wash the skillet. However, all you need is hot water and abrasion (in the form of steel wool or even just sea salt) to clean the skillet, no soap necessary. After you've washed it, set the skillet on the stove and turn on for a minute to make sure all the water has evaporated. Otherwise, you'll find rust spots later. They won't harm you, but you'll have to wash them off before you use the skillet.

Stainless Steel

I have a stainless steel teakettle that has served me faithfully for years. I use it nearly every day. That constant use means that I keep it on the stove, which in turn means it is always stained and splattered by my other cooking. To keep it clean I mix 1 tablespoon of cream of tartar with a couple drops of water to make a liquidy paste. I rub the paste onto the kettle and then wipe it off with a damp cloth. I use this paste to also clean the sides of our toaster and the refrigerator, both stainless steel and magnets for finger-prints, spills, and grime.

Recipes

I'm not a morning person. I don't like to get up before the crack of noon, if I can avoid it. Which means I'm often not one much for breakfast. I prefer my morning meals to be as easy as possi-ble, requiring the least amount of work on my part. When I dis-covered that an easy omelet could be made by scrambling two eggs and then microwaving them on high for two and a half min-utes, my mind was blown. If I were feeling fancy, I would throw some shredded cheese and diced ham in the mix before "nuking" it. I might even take the time while it was cooking to toast some bread. All of a sudden, I had a pretty nutritious meal on my hands. Magick!

However, every meal can't be microwaved omelets. We have to cook other kinds of foods. And to do so, we need instructions.

My first cookbook was the *Better Homes and Gardens New Cook Book*. It was a Christmas gift from my mother the year I moved to the Chicagoland area at the age of nineteen. I still have it, in all its battered, broken-spine glory, and I still use it. But as much as I appreciate the recipes and advice that can be found in those stained and torn pages, I have another cookbook I use more frequently. This cookbook is housed in a binder and contains various printed and handwritten recipes in page protectors. These are recipes I've collected over the years and use monthly. I have filled it with reci-pes that nourish and delight me. These are meals that have become staples over the years, and they are the ones I'll be passing on to my children when they strike out on their own. I'm sharing some of these recipes below, but I am also going to walk you through how to make your own cookbook, filled with meals and recipes that will nourish you.

Creating Your Cookbook

You will need a three-ring binder and sheet protectors that fit it. Over the years I have found this system to be near perfect. That copy of *Better Homes and Gardens* has come completely apart, the binding broken, but my binder just keeps on trucking. The plastic sleeves keep the pages safe from splatters—just wipe them clean. I am able to organize recipes, slip out ones I don't like, and keep everything where I can find it. Best of all, when my children venture out on their own, I'll be able to gift them with their very own cookbooks filled with those recipes they loved. And while I haven't gone quite so far as to add tabs and section dividers yet, that is another way you can organize the cookbook.

 EXERCISE
Consecrate Your Cookbook

To start, you are going to consecrate your new, blank cookbook. Center and ground yourself. Light a candle to Hestia and invite her to join you. Anoint the cover of the binder with your Hestia oil. Visualize the binder full of delicious and nutritious recipes. See yourself flipping through numerous pages, finding the perfect recipe for you and making it, surrounded by all the ingredients you need. Feel the satisfaction that comes from knowing that you not only have all the right tools, but you know how to use them all, and you can make something that feeds not only your body but your soul. And now pour those feelings of satisfaction and abundance into the binder, seeing it radiate.

Filling Your Cookbook

Maybe you already have plenty of recipes that you've made and enjoyed. Transferring them to your new cookbook binder will be an easy task, then. But if you haven't really cooked before or not made any effort to collect the recipes you like in one place, this might take a little bit longer. Feel free to add the recipes that follow. Search the internet for recipes you'd like to try. Ask friends and family for their own tried and true ones. Think about what foods give you comfort, what foods energize you or calm you down. Do you like salty or bitter foods? What meals were you served as a kid that you hated and couldn't stomach? Make sure not to add those to your cookbook. Think beyond just feeling full.

You don't have to write out the recipes from scratch, either. My own binder is filled with printouts from websites, recipes scribbled on torn pieces of notepaper, sticky notes stuck or taped onto computer paper, and cut-outs from packages of graham crackers and whipped cream. The point is to get the recipes in one place so you can use them, not to create a work of art.

When you enter your recipes, add notes on the magickal properties of the ingredients. You might want to even include notes on when you made it and how it made you feel to cook and eat it. What you are creating is a kitchen witchery Book of Shadows. Those notes will help you to choose foods and meals you can cook for certain effects. I have found this to be very helpful in my meal planning. If my family has had a rough day, for example, I am going to choose recipes that include tomatoes to promote feelings of love or recipes that call for a bit of sugar or a squeeze of lemon to increase our happiness.

You shouldn't feel you have to focus solely on food recipes either. Herbal remedies, potions, cocktails, beauty products, cleaning solutions—all of those have a place in your cookbook too if you so choose. Also, you might want to include information like conversion charts, substitution lists, and your favorite recipe websites and even keep a place for local carryout restaurants … just in case you end up not feeling like cooking.

The following recipes are from my own cookbook. I've made them for my family for years. They are nutritious and don't cost much to make. They are also easily adaptable to what you have on hand or what your magickal goals are. You can refer to the ingredient correspondence table in the back of this book to look up the magickal properties of substitutions. Where possible I have added suggestions on how to make the recipes vegetarian or vegan to suit a range of diets.

Granola

Granola sprinkled over yogurt is one of the easiest breakfasts one can make, as long as you have the granola on hand. The ingredients in this recipe bring energies of financial prosperity, success, and love. The oats and clove are used for their money powers, the apple juice taps into loving energies, the vanilla aids in mental powers, and the cinnamon is to bring success to your day. The honey enhances the effectiveness of the other ingredients' magickal properties, while the olive oil taps into the Divine, bringing Hestia (or another deity you are working with) into the mix. The salt adds a bit of protection to those who eat it. All of it together makes for a tasty breakfast.

While I most often use walnuts (for their prosperity magick and because they are most often on hand), you can fine-tune the recipe for very specific types of prosperity through your choice of nuts. Refer to the list of ingredient correspondences for ideas on which nuts to include. Substituting maple syrup for honey will give the granola a focus more on money success, useful if you are look-ing for a raise at work. You can also include additional ingredients like dried raisins (to reinforce the mental magick of the vanilla if you need to succeed on a test or in activities that require thought) or sunflower seeds (to increase your health if your immune system could use a magickal boost). You can add up to 1 cup of additional ingredients to the recipe.

You will need:

> 3 cups rolled oats
>
> 1½ cups nuts
>
> ½ cup apple juice
>
> ½ cup honey (or 100 percent maple syrup)
>
> ¼ cup olive oil
>
> 1 tablespoon vanilla extract
>
> ½ teaspoon cinnamon
>
> ¼ teaspoon cloves
>
> 1 teaspoon sea salt

1. Preheat the oven to 325 degrees Fahrenheit.

2. Combine the oats and nuts.

3. In a saucepan, heat the juice, honey (or maple syrup), oil, and spices.

4. Pour the heated liquid over the oats and nuts.

5. Pour the mixture onto a baking sheet lined with parchment paper and bake 30 to 40 minutes, stirring every 12 to 14 min-utes.

6. Let cool and store in a sealed container.

Muffins

Sometimes what you want is a warm, fresh-baked muffin for breakfast. You might not have the time in the morning to make them from scratch, however. This recipe has the benefit of allowing you to prepare it ahead of time and bake just what you need in the morning. The frozen mix only takes 25 minutes to bake, meaning you can pop a couple into the oven and have a piping-hot breakfast before you have to start your day.

Much like the granola recipe, these muffins take advantage of ingredients with prosperity and success magickal properties. Flour made from wheat provides a base of money energies, and the inclusion of cinnamon (success), sugar (used to attract what you want), and baking powder (an activating ingredient that gives extra power to the other energies in the recipe) make these muffins a prosperity powerhouse, fueling not only your body but also your magickal intentions for the day.

You will need:

> 2 cups flour
>
> 1 teaspoon cinnamon
>
> 2 teaspoons baking powder
>
> ¼ teaspoon salt
>
> ½ cup sugar
>
> 1 egg (or 1 flax egg[30])
>
> ½ cup olive oil or melted butter
>
> 1 cup applesauce
>
> 1 teaspoon vanilla extract

---

30. A flax egg is made by mixing 1 tablespoon flaxseed meal with 2½ tablespoons water.

1. Mix the flour, cinnamon, baking powder, and salt together in a large bowl.

2. In a small bowl, mix together the sugar, egg, oil or melted butter, applesauce, and vanilla extract.

3. Spoon the batter into lined muffin tins.

4. If baking immediately, preheat the oven to 375 degrees Fahrenheit and bake for 20 minutes. Otherwise, place muffin tins in the freezer for an hour. Once frozen, remove the muffin cups from the tins and store in a freezer bag for up to 6 months. When ready to bake, preheat the oven to 375 degrees and bake for 25 minutes.

Lemon Ginger Tea

I don't drink this tea on its own but instead add it to my beverages. It adds a bit of zing that I find invigorating. The ingredients also magickally enhance your tea. The ginger adds energies of success and power, while the lemon blesses you, your drink, and your work. Make a batch and keep it in on hand for when you need a bit of extra support in your endeavors.

You will need:

> 2 lemons, sliced
>
> 2-inch piece of ginger root, sliced

1. Place the lemon and ginger into a 16-ounce mason jar or another glass container.

2. Pour boiling water over the lemon and ginger.

3. Let steep for 20 minutes, then strain out the lemon and ginger.

4. Store the lemon ginger tea in the fridge for up to 2 weeks.

No-Knead Rustic Bread

Bread has been a staple food for centuries. When the United States went into lockdown for the COVID-19 pandemic, one of the foods that was stockpiled was bread. When loaves disappeared from shelves, people turned to the baking aisle and to their ovens, learning to bake bread for themselves. As with the muffins, the wheat in the flour brings magickal energies of money. The addition of yeast, which has properties of growth and transformation, makes a slice of bread the perfect base for any type of financial kitchen witchery.

The following recipe is easy and turns out a couple of loaves. The bread is not as shelf stable as those sold by mass producers. You can freeze half loaves for use later in stuffing and breadcrumb recipes.

You will need:

> 1½ tablespoon active dry yeast
>
> 1 tablespoon salt
>
> 6½ cups all-purpose flour
>
> 3 cups lukewarm water

1. In a large bowl mix the yeast, salt, and water. Stir in flour, mixing so that it is uniformly wet and there are no dry spots. Cover the bowl with a kitchen towel and let the dough rise for 2 to 5 hours.

2. Preheat the oven to 450 degrees Fahrenheit. Divide the dough into two. Place each dough portion into a well-greased oven-safe pan. I usually place one dough lump into my dutch oven and the other into my cast-iron skillet or a bread pan. Let the dough rest for 20 minutes as your oven heats up.

3. Slash the top of the dough, and cover either with the lid of the dutch oven or with tin foil. Place the pan into the oven on the bottom rack. Bake for 20 to 25 minutes. Remove from the oven and let the pan cool for 5 minutes before extracting the loaf to a cooling rack and letting it cool for another 10 minutes. In the meantime, place the second pan in the oven to bake the second loaf of bread.

Pesto

Pesto generally means a sauce made from nuts, oils, cheese, garlic, and basil. I have, over the years, found that I can substitute the basil for any number of leafy greens and end up with a delicious sauce. When basil wasn't available, for instance, I would often use spinach, which I could get in big bags from the grocery store. Pesto is a great dish to make from foraged greens like lamb's-quarters, chickweed, dandelion, and other plants. Going out one spring day to gather greens and then returning home to make pesto for a pasta dish or to eat with crusty bread is a wonderful way to celebrate the return of the growing season. Just make sure you collect plants from places you know are not treated with chemicals.

Magickally, pesto is great for any type of prosperity spells focused on money. From the green color to the basil, which has magickal properties of wealth, this is the sauce you want to eat when you need to bring some extra cash into your pockets. The walnuts bring in properties of abundance, just in case your magickal intentions haven't been clear enough.

This will make two servings of pesto. Each serving can be used with a pound of pasta or can be served as a dip. The recipe freezes well, so you can make several batches when you have a surplus of greens to save for later in the year.

You will need:

½ cup extra-virgin olive oil

⅓ cup walnuts

½ cup grated parmesan cheese

3 cloves garlic, minced

2 packed cups basil or other fresh greens

1. Pour the olive oil into a food processor and add the nuts. Run the food processor until the nuts are chopped.

2. Add the garlic and pulse the food processor a few times.

3. Add the parmesan cheese and blend.

4. Finally, add the greens. You may have to add them in 2 batches and scrape the sides of the food processor as you blend them with the rest of the ingredients.

Vegetable Stock

Vegetable stock is not only a staple but an easy way to make use of any vegetable odds and ends in your fridge. I will often dump celery and carrot tops, the ends of onions, extra sweet pepper slices, and the like into a container in my freezer. I haul the container out once a month and turn all those bits and pieces into a nutritious stock that I can use immediately or freeze, depending on what my needs are.

The key to making stock is to have vegetables that are in 1-inch pieces so as to get as much of the taste and nutrients as possible into the stock. If your odds and ends are too large, give them a chop before dumping them into the pot. You then need to make sure you sauté the vegetables long enough to start the breakdown process but not so long that they burn. Once you've added the water, though, you can let the stock simmer and do its own thing without much attention.

While making this stock from leftover vegetables is the epitome of the scrappy, "make-do" attitude of an idiorhythmic lifestyle, you aren't limited to what you have on hand. If you are starting a venture or looking for a new start, gather fresh, whole vegetables and herbs like the ones listed here for your stock to tap into the energy of new beginnings. You can also change out the suggested herbs. The rosemary, thyme, and bay leaf below all have protective and healing energies. If, perhaps, you want to make a stock that's meant to inspire love, add in some chili peppers and ginger.

You will need:

> 1 large onion
>
> 2 stalks celery, including leaves
>
> 2 large carrots
>
> 1 bunch green onions
>
> 8 cloves garlic
>
> 8 sprigs fresh rosemary (or 1 tablespoon dried leaves)
>
> 8 sprigs fresh thyme (or 1 tablespoon dried leaves)
>
> 1 tablespoon olive oil
>
> 2 bay leaves
>
> 1 teaspoon salt
>
> 2 quarts water

1. Chop the vegetables into 1-inch chunks.
2. Heat oil in a soup pot. Add the vegetables and herbs. Sauté for 5 to 10 minutes. You want the vegetables to be soft, not burnt.
3. Add the salt and water. Bring to a boil, then reduce the heat to a simmer. Let it simmer, uncovered, for 45 minutes to an hour.

4. Strain and discard the vegetables. Use the stock immediately or refrigerate for about 1 week or freeze for 6 months.

Lemon Rosemary Marinade

Use the following marinade to make a dish that brings loving and protective energies to your meal. The rosemary provides the loving magickal properties, while the garlic salt and onion powder add their protection. The lemon acts as a magickal amplifier to the three herbs, while the olive oil holds everything together like Hestia's loving embrace.

This marinade can be used on chicken, or it can be instead drizzled over vegetables before they are roasted. Use freshly squeezed lemon or lemon juice and whole dried rosemary leaves. The amount below works for 1 pound of chicken or 4 cups of vegetables.

You will need:

> 1 teaspoon dried rosemary leaves
>
> 1 teaspoon garlic salt
>
> 1 teaspoon onion powder
>
> ¼ cup olive oil
>
> 2 tablespoons lemon juice

1. Place the rosemary leaves in a mortar and crush them with the pestle. Dried rosemary leaves can be hard and sharp, so you want to break them up so that they'll soften in the cooking process. Add the garlic salt and onion powder.

2. In a separate, small bowl, whisk together the olive oil and lemon juice.

3. Add the spices and whisk to combine.

4. Use on chicken, letting it marinate for 1 hour in the refrigerator, or use it in the following recipe for roasted vegetables.

Roasted Vegetables

Like many of the recipes in this section, this one is meant to be eas-ily altered to suit your tastes and magickal needs. You can change out the vegetables in this recipe with ones of your choice. Cau-liflower, parsnips, sweet potatoes, and brussels sprouts are some you can use instead of or in addition to the ones below. As written, the recipe is focused on vegetables that have healing, calming, and protective magickal properties. This is a dish to feed to your loved ones when you need to foster bonds and love between everyone.

You will need:

> 1 pound potatoes
>
> 2 carrots
>
> 2 stalks celery
>
> 1 medium red onion
>
> Lemon rosemary marinade

1. Cut the potatoes, carrots, and celery into 1-inch chunks. Slice the red onion into ½-inch wide slices.

2. Place the vegetables in a roasting pan and drizzle with the marinade. Stir to evenly coat.

3. Roast the vegetables, covered, at 325 degrees Fahrenheit for 45 minutes, stirring at the 25-minute mark.

4. Increase the oven temperature to 450 degrees. Uncover the pan, stir the vegetables, and roast for another 20 minutes.

10
CLEANING:
A PLACE FOR EVERYTHING
AND EVERYTHING IN ITS PLACE

Let's get this out of the way right now: cleaning, for the most part, is an unpleasant slog. You sweep and vacuum and tidy and dust, and then you have to do it all over again the next day. However, cleaning has been inextricably linked to faith and worship forever. From Buddhist monks sweeping courtyards to committees of women polishing pews, there is an understanding that places of worship need to be clean. As Pagans, working with a deity whose domain is the home, that means our house is also our place of worship. This in turn means we are going to have to do the dishes on a regular basis.

Everyone has a differing definition of clean, or to put it another way, everyone has their own limit of dirty they can live with. In my house, I try to keep counters and tables clutter free and floors swept in the common spaces. When it comes to my children's bedrooms, as long as there are no insects, I don't dictate that they keep it tidy except for the once-a-week pickup so the floor can be vacuumed. You and your household will have to decide where on the spectrum—from interior design magazine slick to artist-in-residence cluttered—you want your home to occupy. Your goal is a level of cleanliness that is maintainable and that keeps your house from being a health hazard.

Unless you are living by yourself, household chores should not fall on your shoulders alone. Everyone who lives in the household should help clean. Even young children can be tasked with simple chores like picking up their toys and making their beds. Taking the time to sit down with your family to decide what tasks need to be done and who will do them can help avoid any fights over who is supposed to take out the garbage.

In this chapter I'll be going over what one needs to clean the house, how to make household cleaners (and why you may want to), and how to set up a cleaning schedule. This may seem like the least magickal of all the chapters. At least with cooking there's an established tradition of kitchen witchery one can look to for inspiration, whereas cleaning… well, cleaning is drudgery.

However, much like the idea of creating rituals for entering and leaving your home, cleaning gives you the opportunity to really get to know your home. Each house, each apartment, each cottage, and each mansion all have their own quirks and special energies. There might be a corner that's always cold. Is it because the insulation is missing there because the builder was cheap and was trying to cut costs? Or is it because a spirit resides there? What is the building's default energy level? Is it usually tranquil? Or does it always have an underlying hum of action? How would you know if it is always buried under the energies of the people living there, the magick you perform, and the helping spirits, household spirits and deities that might also be living there?

Cleaning your home brings you into regular contact with both the physical and metaphysical sides of the space. The familiarity that will come from this will aid you in any spellwork you do that targets your home, find what places in your home are best suited for activities like meditation and relaxation, and reveal what genius loci might be residing. And, once you have a good feel for the general atmosphere of your home, you'll be more likely to know sooner if something is off due to magickal interference (from being targeted by a hex, for example).

So, yes, cleaning might not be as glamorous as other forms of spellwork, but it is vital. With that in mind, let's dive in.

Cleaning Tools

With regard to the tools needed for cleaning, you don't need much. Pretty much any kind of broom and mop will do. Pick one that suits your budget. For a broom, I'm talking about a working broom, not a besom used in spellwork, although you can use your broom as a besom if you wish. I have a cheap squeeze mop, which I use a bit differently than would be expected, as you'll find down below. You'll need a dustpan and if you have carpeting, a vacuum as well.

You can cut up old t-shirts for rags. Not only does this keep them out of landfills, but the cotton of worn t-shirts is nonabrasive and absorbent. Keeping a stack on hand means you'll always have rags for cleanup that can then be thrown in the wash. You'll need an abrasive scrubber of some sort. There are plenty of sustainable options out there, like scrubbers made from hemp, bamboo, plant cellulose, and even coconut and walnut. If you have any cast-iron dishes, you'll want a steel wool scrubber as well.

For dusting you can use the rags, but a wand duster will help you with hard-to-reach spots, books on the shelf, and underneath furniture on hardwood floors. I've developed two techniques to help with the tediousness of dusting. First I've come to regard dust as the physical manifestation of stale and stagnant energy. If I can see dust, then it means it's time for a cleansing. This is especially true of our family altar as it means I've been neglecting it. Second, after I have run my lambswool duster over everything, I'll take it outside and whack against a pole while yelling, "Get the fuck out!" at the bad energy trapped with the dust. It is very cathartic, and I recommend everyone try it at least once, although I'll caution you to try not to break the duster.

On the subject of dusting, use lint rollers to dust fabric and paper lampshades. An old sock worn over the hand will make dusting window blinds easier. And if you have a ceiling fan, use a pillowcase to dust it by opening the pillowcase and placing it over each individual blade. By then pulling the case off the blade, you'll pull the dust off as well and it will fall into the pillowcase rather than drifting down on your head.

Homemade Cleaning Supplies

Making cleaning solutions allows you to be environmentally conscious. Most natural cleaners involve ingredients such as vinegar, baking soda, and lemons. The components are biodegradable and nontoxic to people, plants, and animals.

Homemade cleaners are also cheaper than mass-produced ones. Even the outlay at the beginning in spray bottles and containers can be offset by reusing ones you already have on hand. When you finish a bottle of window cleaner, you can wash it out and reuse it.

It's not just environmental concerns. You can add moon water or essential oils to your store-bought cleaners. Magickally speaking, though, man-made chemicals are going to have their own energies and powers that aren't well understood. There is, I think, a real risk of creating a concoction that doesn't work, or worse, causes harm. To that end, I rather err on the side of caution.

Last, most of the stains and dirt you are going to be dealing with everyday won't require harsh cleaning supplies. If you keep up with a cleaning schedule in your house, you'll rarely ever need anything harsher than dishwashing soap when dealing with stains. You may have to apply a bit of elbow grease, but as long as you use the right tools (stainless steel wool, rags, microfiber cloths) and clean up stains when they happen, you'll be able to deal with 99 percent of cleaning problems.

Note: What's up with the dish soap? After reading through the above you might wonder why the recipes that follow include dish soap, which isn't known for being the greenest of cleaners. Soap bonds with water and grease and oil, making a solution that can be washed away. Grease and oil can't be cleaned with just water.

Nearly all liquid dish soaps contain chemicals that have varying deleterious effects on the environment. One option is to use castile soap, which is made from vegetable oils and lye. Unfortunately, castile soap and vinegar (one of the main ingredients in many of the recipes because of its dirt-fighting abilities) don't play well together. Fortunately, the recipes below don't require much dish soap, so a single bottle can go a long way.

To lessen the impact of dish soaps, you can look for products that don't contain phosphates or triclosan. Also, you can look at the Environmental Working Group's website (www.ewg.org /guides/cleaners), where they have rated cleaning products on their environmental impact. There you can look for brands that have an A rating (on a scale of A to F), which indicates they have the least amount of harmful chemicals.

Cleaning Routine and Timing

A routine cleaning schedule should work for you. Scheduling chores on days when you don't have the time for them or listing chores that you don't find important (cleaning the baseboards, for example) is going to work against your sense of peace and well-being in a place where you need those two feelings the most. So if cobwebs in the ceiling corners don't bother you, why would you schedule daily dusting sessions? Better to attend to the chore only when the cobwebs are tickling the top of your head.

Cleaning routines can be broken down into four categories: daily, weekly, monthly, and seasonally. There's a breakdown of what each category involves. Read through them and think about your own situation and life to come up with a cleaning routine that works for you. At the very basic, you can decide what tasks need to be done each day, go through the Full Moon House Cleansing at the end of this chapter, and engage in a spring and fall cleaning for all the rest.

Daily

Daily cleaning involves those chores that keep the home tidy and ensure that the larger cleaning jobs aren't as difficult. These include chores like dishes, making the bed, wiping down counters, sweeping floors, and tidying up.

Sweep dirt out the front door for major house cleanings. But if you can't, sweep with intention toward your garbage can and then dump your dustpan. This gets the negative or stale energy out of your domain. This works best if the garbage can has a lid, as that serves as a boundary between the home space and the garbage space.

Keep an empty basket to use when you are tidying up around the house. Items that aren't in the proper place can be placed in the basket and conveyed to their appropriate locations.

Weekly

Weekly chores are those larger jobs that don't have to be done every day: mopping or vacuuming floors, scrubbing the tub and toilet, and so on. Some might depend on outside factors when it comes to scheduling. For example cleaning out your refrigerator should happen before you go grocery shopping, or taking out the trash might need to wait until the routine trash collection days. You can either do them all at once or spread them throughout the week so you don't get overwhelmed.

Monthly

Monthly cleaning tasks involve those bigger jobs that really, honest-to-goodness need to be done, just not *right* now. I'm talking about cleaning the microwave and oven, washing windows and mirrors, scrubbing out the garbage can, and the like. As with weekly cleaning, you could schedule all these monthly chores at one time. Or break them up throughout the month—perhaps scheduling them during the new waxing quarter, full, and waning quarter moons—so you aren't spending several hours scouring surfaces.

Your altar(s) should be getting attention at least once a month as well. Take the time to really clean that space: dust everything, recharge crystals or other talismans and charms, change out the altar cloth, toss incense ash, and refresh any used-up spell components that might have gathered there throughout the month. Once you've cleaned your altar space, cleanse and bless it with a smoke or spray cleanse.

Seasonally

Seasonal cleaning involves mostly vertical surfaces: walls, doors, cabinet fronts, and outside windows, all the spaces that get dirty so slowly and over such a length of time that we don't really notice until we've cleaned them. Dust and straighten picture frames, use a cleaning solution over the walls and kitchen cabinets, and perhaps even give the baseboards some attention if you are so inclined. Open up the windows, if even for only a few moments to get fresh air into your home to break up any stagnant energy. This is the time you should be renewing any protective spells on the house if you haven't done so in a while. Sprinkle baking soda over your carpets and let sit for ten minutes before vacuuming it up. The baking soda will absorb any odors that have settled into the fibers.

A note on the emotional side of cleaning: When you start cleaning your home ritually, you may find that it stirs up unpleasant thoughts, old trauma, or doubts. This can happen especially if you haven't made a habit of cleaning before. Take your time when cleaning, take breaks if you begin to feel overwhelmed, and make sure to drink plenty of water as you clean. Once you have finished, you might want to take a cleansing bath or shower to wash away any negativity that came up and has attached to you.

Full Moon House Cleansing

Cleaning your home is important for your physical well-being, but it can also help with your mental health and mood. And while cleaning and cleansing can often be linked, the two are not mutually inclusive. Cleansing requires attention and effort beyond the physical act. You might not want to go through the effort of invoking magick every time you do the dishes. In that case, I've included a house cleansing/cleaning ritual you can do on the full moon.

If I do nothing else beyond my daily tidying up and wiping down of counters, I will take the time on the day of the full moon to do this ritual. It serves to reinforce the connection I have with my home, seeing it not just as where I keep my things, watch TV, and sleep, but as my shelter. It connects me to the energies of the moon, Hestia, and feelings of love and comfort, and it provides a bit of routine in a life that rarely has structure.

You will need the lemon rosemary water from page 174, sea salt, dusting and mop rags, a broom or vacuum cleaner, and a mop.

Tidy up the house. Put things where they belong, hang up coats, and put away shoes. Use a duster or rag to dust surfaces. Pour about a cup or more of sea salt into a bowl. Hold the bowl in your receptive hand, hover your dominant hand over the bowl, and charge the salt by seeing white light cascading from your dominant hand into the salt. Scatter the salt over your floors while saying, "That which would harm me, chase it away; that which would hold me back, chase it away; that which would sicken me, chase it away." Visualize the salt burning away any negativity, bad energy, and so on.

Sweep your floors, moving toward the door to the outside. Do the same as you vacuum. Dispose of the sweepings outdoors, in the compost, or in the trash, and empty the vacuum. Open the windows, bringing in fresh air to clear away any remaining negative or harmful energies.

Now it's time to mop the floor. If there is any salt left over from earlier, add that and the lemon rosemary water to your mop water. Visualize the protective and purifying energies of the lemon rosemary water settling into your floor and shielding your home from any hostile, exterior influences. For carpeted areas, you can wet your fingers with the lemon rosemary water and flick it over the floor, making sure to get into corners.

Pour the rest of the lemon rosemary water down all the drains. Also add some to each toilet and then flush it. Don't forget any basement drains. Those are often overlooked access points that are left forgotten when we are casting protective spells on the various points of entrance to our homes.

Put away your cleaning tools and supplies and toss any rags or sponges into the wash. Close the windows if you haven't done so already. Drink a glass of water. Your home is now cleansed.

Cleaning Recipes

Make the following recipes during the waning moon to include its banishing properties to your cleaning products. I also like to add moon water to my cleaning products, just to give the magickal cleansing aspects a boost. You don't need a lot—a tablespoon will do.

Tub Cleaner

You will need:

> 1 cup white vinegar
>
> 1 cup dish soap

Pour vinegar and dish soap into a spray bottle. Shake to mix. To use:

1. Spray down the tub, shower walls, shower door, etc.

2. Let sit for 30 minutes.

3. Wipe away and rinse with water.

Store the tub cleaner in a cool, dark place. Shake every time before use. This cleaner can also be used for cleaning sinks, countertops, and even the toilet. (*Note:* if your tub is an older porcelain one, skip this cleaner. While vinegar is a mild acid, it is still strong enough to pit the surface. Instead, simply use 3 tablespoons of dish soap mixed in 1 gallon of hot water. Use a soft rag to scrub the porcelain surface and rinse with clean water.)

It will have a strong vinegar smell that will dissipate after a while. You can alleviate the scent by adding a few drops of essential oil or using vinegar in which lemon peels have been soaked.

Add 1 tablespoon of rosewater or 10 drops of rose essential oil to the spray to infuse it with loving energies, especially if you need to work on self-love. Add 10 drops of lavender essential oil if you need more relaxing energies in your bathroom. This is helpful if you are in the habit of taking a bath before bedtime. For general good health energies, add 10 drops of tea tree or eucalyptus essential oil.

Carpet Cleaner

You will need:

    2 cups water

    1 tablespoon white vinegar

    1 tablespoon dish soap

In a spray bottle mix the water, vinegar, and dish soap. To use:

1. First, clean up any solid material from the carpet and soak up any pooled liquid.
2. Sprinkle baking soda onto the stain and let it sit for 10 minutes to absorb any smells from the stain. Vacuum up the baking soda.
3. Spray the carpet cleaner onto the remaining stain and work it into the carpet with a brush.

4. Blot it up with a clean white rag until all the liquid has been absorbed.

5. Use a new, wet rag to sponge off any remaining carpet cleaner and then blot to dry.

Store in a cool, dark place. Shake the bottle before each use to mix the components.

I don't advise adding essential oils to this cleaner, as they could stain the carpet you're trying to clean. Moon water can be added, however.

Floor Cleaner

You will need:

> 1 cup white vinegar
>
> 1 cup baking soda
>
> 1 tablespoon dish soap
>
> 2 gallons hot water

Mix the components in a bucket or the sink. To use:

1. Have a stack of rags on hand as well as a bucket (or the other sink if you have a two-sink situation in your kitchen), and grab your mop.

2. Drop a rag into the floor wash, and wring it out so that it is wet but not dripping.

3. Spread the rag out on the floor and use the mop to scrub the area until the rag is no longer wet.

4. Toss the spent rag into the bucket or empty sink, grab a fresh cloth, and repeat the process until the floor is clean.

This process takes a bit more effort than just plunging the mop into the cleaner and scrubbing away at the floor. It has the advantage, however, of keeping the solution free of debris. You aren't constantly dipping a dirty mop back into the water that is supposed to be cleaning your floor. The dirty rags can then be tossed into the wash.

Add salt to the floor cleaner for its purification and blessing properties. Peppermint essential oil has antibacterial and antifungal properties, as well as being associated with love. Pine essential oil is a germ killer as well as being effective against mold and mildew. Its magickal powers of money make it a useful addition to the floor cleaner if you want to bring more prosperity in terms of money into your home.

Spiritual floor washes are found in Conjure and Hoodoo/Rootwork. Some premade floor washes can be purchased and come with instructions on their use (which may include washing over a set number of days and reciting psalms). My floor cleaner recipe is not the same thing as those floor washes. If you want to use a spiritual floor wash in your house, look to a reputable practitioner for supplies and instruction.

Window Cleaner

You will need:

- 1¼ cup distilled water
- ½ cup 80-proof vodka
- ¼ cup white vinegar
- 8 to 10 drops of an essential oil of your choice (or see suggestions on the next page)

Pour all components into a spray bottle and shake to mix. Use as you would any glass cleaner. Store the cleaner in a cool, dry place and shake well before use.

Windows, like doors, provide entrance into a house both physically and magickally. And yet, we'll often focus on warding or protecting doors and ignoring the windows. Cleaning your windows regularly gives you the opportunity to refresh the protective spells on your house.

When you are cleaning windows and mirrors, use lint-free rags or newspaper to wipe down and dry the glass to reduce streaking.

The essential oils in this recipe are not only added for their magickal properties, but they are necessary for the cleaner to work. Lemon essential oil is a good, all-purpose oil to use for this cleaner, as its protective properties turn away harmful spells and the evil eye. Basil essential oil is good to use for blessing your home. Spearmint can be added if your house has gone through a round of the flu to bring healing energies into the home. You can also play around with different combinations of essential oils to create more complex magickal solutions for your window cleaning.

Microwave Cleaner

You will need:

> 1 lemon
>
> ½ cup of water

Pour water into a microwave-safe container (a coffee mug works just fine). Slice a lemon in half. Squeeze the lemon into the water and then drop in the lemon halves.

To use, microwave the container for 3 minutes and then let sit for 5 minutes. The steam from the water and the oils from the lemon will coat the inside of the microwave, loosening any stuck on food and stains.

Using a clean rag, wipe down the inside of the microwave. You can dip it into the lemon water if needed to scrub away anything that is still sticking. Then dry with a clean rag and you're done.

Oven Cleaner

You will need:

> 2 cups water
> ½ cup vinegar
> Baking soda
> Sea salt

To use:

1. Remove the oven racks and set aside to be cleaned separately.
2. Fill a spray bottle with water and vinegar. Spray the inside of the oven as well as the inside of the door liberally. You want it wet enough so that the baking soda and sea salt will stick to everything.
3. Sprinkle baking soda on the walls, bottom, and inside of the oven door. Follow this with the sea salt, and make sure you have a thick layer.
4. Spray everything again to start the reaction between the vinegar and baking soda. If the oven is particularly dirty, you can leave everything overnight. Otherwise, use a scrubber to scrub the oven.
5. Use the spray to help remove everything and wipe the oven down with dry rags.

You can clean the oven racks using the same method.

I don't recommend using essential oils when cleaning the oven. However, you can use moon water, the lemon rosemary water, or even vinegar in which lemon peels have been soaked to make the spray solution.

Ideally, the oven gets cleaned once a month. But if we were going to be living in an ideal world, the oven would clean itself magickally, without any effort on our part. My oven gets cleaned less often than that, based on the season (in the hotter months I don't use it as much, so it stays cleaner than the colder months). With that in mind, know that no one is expecting you to whistle while you clean the burnt cheese and grease stains in the oven. If you really hate the task, you can channel that emotion into your scrubbing, which can, at times, be a bit cathartic.

Laundry

Laundry is probably the household chore that requires the most energy and cleaning supplies. Making your own laundry soap isn't going to cut down on the time it takes to do laundry. But, as with all the rest of the recipes here, it does give you greater control over what kind of energies might get soaked into the fibers of your clothes. The recipe below depends on the alkaline and water-softening properties of the components to clean fabric. It is not a true detergent, and so clothes with serious stains (blood, grass, dirt, etc.) will need to be pretreated before laundering. The upside, however, is it is the gentlest laundry cleaner, and none of the ingredients are harmful to the environment.

You will need:

>   1½ cup baking soda
>   1½ cup washing soda
>   ½ cup Epsom salt

¼ cup sea salt

20 drops of essential oil

Mix the sodas and salts together and place in a glass container that has a lid (mason jars work well). Add in the essential oil, close the container, and shake it to distribute the essential oil throughout the mixture.

Just like with the window cleaner, you have a lot of freedom with which essential oils you can use in the laundry detergent. Tea tree oil is good for its antibacterial and antifungal properties. Use eucalyptus for its healing magickal properties or rose to imbue your family's clothes with loving energies. If you are trying to increase your prosperity, add peppermint or basil to the detergent.

Use 1 tablespoon of the laundry detergent for regular and lightly soiled loads. For larger loads or for clothes that are heavily soiled, use 2 tablespoons.

You can add vinegar to the fabric softener dispenser to help soften fabric and reduce static cling.

While hanging your clothes outside is the most ecologically friendly way to dry them, that's not possible all the time for everyone. Adding wool dryer balls to your loads will not only help with softening clothes and static cling, but it will also reduce drying time. If you are still having issues with staticky clothes, place 2 to 3 large safety pins in a rag and add it to the dry cycle as well.

Note: What is washing soda? Washing soda is a salt like baking soda, but it has a higher alkalinity. The washing soda works by softening water, which allows it to better penetrate fabric, and it binds with soil that has been lifted out of clothes.

While washing soda can be purchased in the store or online, you can make it at home from baking soda. To do so, pour 2 cups of baking soda in a shallow baking tray or dish. Spread it out into a thin layer. Bake at 400 degrees Fahrenheit for an hour. Stir the baking soda and then spread out again; this ensures an even distribution of heat. Bake another hour. Remove from the oven and let cool. The resulting powder will be not as fine as baking soda and will be a different color. Store in an airtight container.

Lemon Rosemary Water

This cleaning solution is different from the others in this chapter. It is meant for spiritual and metaphysical cleaning and purification. It can be used as a window and door wash, in protection and purification rituals, and to dress candles and in spells.

You will need:

2 lemons

4 sprigs rosemary or 1 tablespoon dried rosemary leaves

Pinch of sea salt

Water

Fill a medium saucepan with 4 cups of water. Slice the lemons and add them along with the rosemary and sea salt to the pan. Bring the water to a boil. Reduce the heat and simmer for 20 minutes. Turn off the heat and let the water cool. Once it is cool, strain out the herbs, and store the water in a jar in the refrigerator for up to 2 weeks.

11
CREATING YOUR OWN WHEEL OF THE YEAR

In 2018 a New Zealand boy invented a holiday, Wolfenoot. The holiday celebrates the spirit of wolves and those who are kind to dogs. His mother posted about it on Facebook and it took off. People's desire for a wholesome festivity absent the baggage that comes with more established holidays meant that by the next year people all over the world were celebrating Wolfenoot.

Why am I writing about a child's holiday in a book on Hestia? Because, at their core, all holidays are made up. The progression of the seasons, the phases of the moon, and the rising and setting of the sun are constant. Everything else is an invention of the human mind. However, holidays and the marking of time serve a very important function of organization, which falls in the domain of Hestia.

My family, for example, celebrates the winter solstice, which falls between the 20th and the 23rd of December. We also observe Ice Cream for Breakfast (the first Saturday of February). Every full moon that we are able we kindle a fire in our firepit and perform magick. We celebrate Halloween and birthdays each year. And Thanksgiving is a full four days broken into distinct celebrations (Thanksgiving, the Eatening, Thanksgaming, and the Eatening II).

Our calendar has been built to accommodate the fact that our daughter splits her time between two households, our Pagan beliefs, and my witchcraft. We have spent years boiling our celebrations down to a core that makes us happy and helps us mark the passage of the year. This section of *The Scent of Lemon & Rosemary* aims to help you do the same.

Marking the passage of time and celebrating milestones, anniversaries, and events has been a part of being human since the beginning. The movement of stars and planets, the cycling of seasons, and even the movements of animals have been used throughout history to help us make sense of the passage of time. The regular movement of these natural phenomena have led countless cultures and religions to view time as a cycle, not only when it comes to the succession of one season after another, but also with regard to ideas of reincarnation, the afterlife, death, and birth.

One of the first-known calendars is the Ishango bone. This baboon fibula—at least 11,000 years old and discovered on the border of Uganda and the Democratic Republic of Congo—bears columns of notches that have been theorized to track the lunar cycle, perhaps as a menstruation or agricultural tool.[31]

The human focus on dates and time has led us to discover smaller and more precise units of time measurement and to specify days for every conceivable occasion (see the previously mentioned Ice Cream for Breakfast Day). Time, clearly, is important, but just how it should be counted and observed can be less understood, especially for Pagans living in a society that is built around Christian holidays. There is no reason Pagans and witches can't

---

31. Claudia Zaslavsky, "Women as the First Mathematicians," *International Study Group on Ethnomathematics Newsletter* 7, no. 1 (January 1992): n.p., https://web.nmsu.edu/~pscott/isgem71.htm.

celebrate Christmas, July Fourth, or other national holidays. But maybe you object to Thanksgiving because of its emphasis on stereotypical and false narratives based around the colonization of the Americas. Or maybe you are comfortable with Christmas because of its emphasis on commercialism. Maybe you want to create or find holidays that are more in line with your beliefs and morals. Whatever the reason, there is nothing stopping you from creating your own Wheel of the Year.

Holidays can be difficult. They can be awash in expectations. They can engender feelings of guilt or fear. They can be used to further government agendas.

But that's not what holidays should be. They are meant not only to mark the passage of time, but also to deepen our connection: to our world, to our beliefs, to each other, and to ourselves, depending on the festivity. To that end, there is nothing stopping you from picking and choosing from various federal or Pagan holidays to celebrate or even making some up.

Paganism is an earth-centered belief system. As such, many of the holidays and even the calendar used by Pagans are based around the seasons and the moon cycle. Solstices, equinoxes, and the full moon all play significant roles in various Pagan calendars and influence the timing of magick spells and rituals. The Wheel of the Year is one such calendar that consists of eight events linked to the sun's movements. The festivals of Yule and Litha fall on the winter and summer solstices, respectively. Ostara and Mabon are the spring and fall equinoxes. And the holidays Imbolc, Beltane, Lughnasadh, and Samhain all fall between the aforementioned holidays.

The holidays are adopted from various other calendars, mostly Celtic, by Wiccans and early Neopagans. They have roots in natural events, such as the start of ewes giving birth around Imbolc, that mark the beginnings of seasons.

The Wheel of the Year was codified in the middle of the twentieth century and is widespread among various Wiccan, Druid, and other Pagan groups. There have been hundreds of books, thousands of articles, and hundreds of thousands if not millions of webpages written on the Wheel of the Year, its celebrations, and ways to observe them. The goal of this section is not to go over territory explored already but to investigate the process of building your own calendar.

Holidays fall into one of two categories: external and internal. The difference between the two is only a matter of scope. External holidays are ones that are shared by groups of people. Your community and government might recognize these days officially, closing down different institutions or businesses (think post office or bank closings) to mark the holiday. The celebration might not be state sanctioned but still celebrated by many people (Valentine's Day, for example). Internal holidays are those that are personal and celebrated only by you or perhaps your close family and friends.

In our home, for example, the Saturday after Thanksgiving is known as Thanksgaming and is devoted to board and card games and eating leftovers. Some years we've opened our house to friends and family on that day. Others it's just been myself, my husband, and our two children who gather around the table for pie and Munchkin.

Your calendar can be a mix of external and internal celebrations. Add as many or as few as you want. The point is to create something that is meaningful to you that helps you feel connected with yourself and with those you love.

EXERCISE 1
Creating Your Personal Wheel of the Year

This exercise will take a couple of hours. You can do it on your own, but if you are part of a family, you might want to include them. Initially, plan an evening or an afternoon. You'll need a pencil, paper, and a calendar, at the very least. You can also gather markers, stickers, sticky tabs, highlighter pens, or whatever other supplies that will help you tap into your creativity.

Start by lighting a candle and inviting Hestia to the exercise with the words, "Hestia, as you ensure the proper ordering of the household, assist me in putting the right ordering of my cycle of time." Sit for a moment, focusing on the flame until you feel her presence. I usually feel her as a comforting presence at my right shoulder, but you may experience her presence in the candle's heat or a scent of cinnamon or in some other way.

Once ready, start with listing all the holidays that are important to you. Don't worry about putting them in order or when they happen; just brainstorm and list them. Include everything that helps you feel good and connected. We're not adding holidays that stress you out. Nor should you include any holidays you've observed out of peer or familial pressure. Have a strained or nonexistent relationship with your father? Don't add Father's Day just because you are "supposed" to celebrate it. You are creating a life and home that is a safe and welcoming space, and your calendar is going to reflect that.

Once you've listed everything, turn to a new sheet of paper. This is where you are going to put your brainstormed list in order. Using the calendar and the internet, write down the holidays in order, with their dates. You can add an extra layer of organization by color coding holidays according to their category: birthdays, anniversaries, official, personal, religious, and magickal holidays. On a new sheet of paper draw an equilateral cross. Starting at the top right of the paper, label each section: winter, spring, summer, fall.

Write your holidays in the various boxes as they fall into the seasons. You can use the calendar definition of the seasons (December/January/February = winter, March/April/May = spring, June/July/August = summer, September/October/November = fall), or if your local community or culture uses different dates, use those (for example, summer's start could be linked instead to the last date of frost, as this is when crops would be planted out of doors).

Take a moment to look over your chart. Anything missing? If so, add it, if you realize later that you omitted a holiday, or you later decide to add a celebration, you can add it in. Your Wheel of the Year is going to be a living document.

Now you are going to tap into your inner creativity. Decorate your Wheel. Add stickers or pictures to illustrate the holidays, color it, draw on it. This is a sacred document you've made, so fancy it up as it deserves: think illuminated manuscripts, temple mosaics, and pictographs. Art can't be separated from the human experience. It doesn't matter if you don't view yourself as artistic. It is the effort and expression that matter.

Now you have a blueprint for your personal Wheel of the Year. It's time to implement it practically. Get out your calendar or planner and insert your holidays. You might want to research and add events like the coming year's full moons, eclipses (solar and lunar), and any astrological events for magickal planning. If you have family members, either post a calendar where everyone can see it or include them on any digital calendar you keep by inviting them to add the events to their own.

Many cultures recognized fall as the end of the year and winter as the start of the new year. This was based on agricultural necessities, with the fall harvest being the end of the cycle and winter being the beginning of the next. These same cultures counted the end of the day and the beginning of the next at dusk, rather than midnight. You can orientate your personal Wheel of the Year in a way that makes sense for you. For this exercise I am going to be working with winter as the start of the year.

EXERCISE 2
Creating Your Personal Wheel of the Year

An alternative to exercise 1 is to take a yearlong approach. Again, you'll need a calendar, either printed or electronic. As the year progresses, you'll mark on your calendar any holidays, anniversaries, or celebrations you take part in. Once a year has passed, you'll look over the calendar to compile your master list of holidays and dates. While this process takes longer and requires a greater amount of dedication and effort on your part, it can result in a more accurate calendar, as you'll be listing events you know you want to observe and have observed rather than perhaps including holidays that you later realize aren't important to you.

No matter which exercise you decide on, keep in mind you can alter your Wheel of the Year as time goes on. In fact, it is a good idea to review your list every once in a while (perhaps every other year or at least every five years) to evaluate if it is still relevant to your life.

EXERCISE 3
Creating Your Personal Wheel of the Year

Once you have a template for your personal Wheel of the Year, you are going to flesh out the ritual and magickal dates. We are taught by our cultures how to celebrate dates like national and community holidays, birthdays, and the like. When you're dealing with personal or magickal holidays, you want to have a "script" you've thought about and recorded beforehand. This way you aren't facing the full moon wanting to celebrate it but having no clue what you want to do.

Give yourself another evening or afternoon and look at your dates on the calendar that don't have a tradition behind their celebration. Consider why you include that date on your personal Wheel of the Year. Why is it important to you? What activities do you want to do on that day? What are your goals? What do you need for the day? Visualize what the perfect celebration would look, smell, sound, taste, and feel like. Reality rarely lives up to our ideal fantasies, but that doesn't mean we don't imagine the best-case scenario. If you keep a Book of Shadows, you can record your thoughts there. Otherwise, keep your notes somewhere, on a sticky note stuck to the relevant month on the calendar or as a detail on the date in your electronic calendar. If you need to gather materials, make supplies, or otherwise need planning time for the celebration, make sure to mark a date far enough in advance that you will have time to prepare.

Keep in mind that holidays and celebrations don't have to be elaborate to be meaningful. Going outside and gazing on the moon each month when it is full is as meaningful as a carefully choreographed ritual with props, singing, and a feast. The point of this chapter is to create something that fits your life and resonates with you.

12
MODERN VALUES:
LIVING JUSTLY IN AN UNJUST WORLD

We have spent a lot of time exploring the microcosm of the home as the domain of Hestia. Expanding the lens to look at our society allows us to see how her concerns encompass the wider world. The phrase "As above, so below" comes into play here. Change starts in the home and with the individual, and yet one can't have a stable home environment if the surrounding area is polluted. The two are inextricably entwined. A witch working magick draws upon energies and calls on spirits that occupy a greater plane than their personal sphere. We cannot do so and also insist that our responsibilities stop at our front doors.

In chapter 1 I explained how Hestia is the goddess of the senate, that she advocates self-rule and social justice and is anti-capitalist. This understanding of her outward-facing aspect underlies this chapter. Three relevant topics covered here are environmentalism, cultural appropriation, and consumerism. All three are concepts that would most likely not have been understandable to the people who first started worshipping Hestia and placing her in her honored position. However, they do all fall under her sphere of influence.

The theme of this chapter could be summed up as "ruthlessly interrogate your beliefs and actions." Or maybe it is "do the required reading." If we can spend time and energy on reading books and articles and blog posts about deities, what days are best for timing a money spell, ways to celebrate Midsummer, and how one can tell a green witch from a kitchen witch, we should be able to put in the same amount of work into making sure our practices are sustainable and ethical. Research and learning are fundamental to being a Pagan and a witch, as neither are a major part of dominant cultures. We are required to search out information if we want to know what it means to be one or the other.

We need to understand that the environmentalism of the 1970s is not suited for the twenty-first century. We need to face the appropriative origins of modern Paganism and witchcraft. And we need to come to terms with the part we play in capitalism. All of these are topics that are uncomfortable, especially if you are white or otherwise benefit from privileges that minority populations don't. If we aren't willing to do the hard work, however, then can we really call ourselves Pagans and witches?

Environmentalism

It is clear that the days of reduce, reuse, and recycle to save the planet are past. Scientists and nearly all governments the world over agree that we've reached a crisis point with regard to global warming. Drastic action has to be taken or else the human race is going to suffer greatly in the very near future and may even go extinct entirely.

For years the bulk of the responsibility for this growing crisis has been placed on the shoulders of the individual. People have been told to turn off lights, to recycle their paper, and to turn to reusable shopping bags to reduce their carbon footprint. While these ideas are good in fostering an attitude of environmentalism and awareness of our interaction with the earth, they don't address the main culprits in climate change. In 2017 the Carbon Majors Report found that only 100 companies account for 71 percent of global emissions.[32]

Corporations, and the governments that facilitate them, need to be held accountable. Boycotts, petitions, and letter writing campaigns have proven to be effective at times. Electing officials who promote acts like the Green New Deal, who work to protect the environment, and who pass laws that keep companies in check is going to be even more effective. And those tools can feel overwhelming and pointless at times.

When we are faced with that reality, it can be easy to wonder just how much of a difference individual life choices can make. When those doubts creep in, we turn back to the concept of "As above, so below" and Hestia's influence over the hearth and the state. We practice personal environmentalism as a prayer, act of faith, and, yes, even magick done on the microcosmic level to change the macrocosm.

Being Environmentally Smart

In 2018 the picture of a plastic straw being removed from a turtle's nostril became the poster image of the straw ban. People were eager to save the ocean and its adorable inhabitants. United States businesses, cities, and states began to ban the use of plastic straws. Alternatives of metal, bamboo, paper, and even pasta were offered up in dozens of articles and blog posts. The move was made out of the best intentions, and it encapsulates perfectly the thoughtlessness of many solutions to the problem of pollution.

32. Paul Griffin, "CDP Carbon Majors Report 2017," the Carbon Majors Database, July 2017, https://b8f65cb373b1b7b15feb-c70d8ead6ced550b4d987d7 c03fcdd1d.ssl.cf3.rackcdn.com/cms/reports/documents/000/002/327 /original/Carbon-Majors-Report-2017.pdf?1499691240.

The fact is that plastic bags are a greater threat to marine life than plastic straws. A ban on single-use bags would have a greater impact than a straw ban. However, removing such plastic bags from our lives would require a greater shift in our habits, and people often don't want to sacrifice convenience, even for cute turtles. Banning straws is also ableist. Many people need straws to drink because of medical conditions. For some the offered straw alternatives aren't workable solutions. And so we leave the vulnerable behind in our rush to prove how green we are. A better response would be to just forgo the plastic straw if you don't require one.

This is where our environmentalism needs to actually be effective, rather than just for show. We need to constantly evaluate what we are doing against criteria on its larger impact, not only on us, but on populations that might suffer because of them. People with disabilities, minorities, the poor, women, and others are not acceptable losses in the struggle to heal the planet.

Responsible Recycling

Recycling is one of those feel-good activities that a great number of people do wrong. Many will toss a plastic container into the bin without a thought toward whether or not it is actually recyclable, if the recycling company takes that type of plastic, or even if it is in the proper state to be recycled.

Going back to plastic bags: they cannot be recycled by most companies. Tossing them into your recycle bin will just gum up the works for the company, costing them time and money which could either lead them to raising prices or even closing down. There are companies that can recycle plastic bags, and they get their material from bins outside of grocery stores. So instead of just tossing them into the bin, you'll need to collect them and make a trip to the store. Another alternative is to hand your collected bags over to your local food bank. Single-use plastic bags are used an average of only twelve minutes before they are discarded.[33] Providing them to food banks helps extend that lifespan. If you are feeling particularly crafty, you can even make plarn—yarn made out of plastic bags—to craft various items.

Look into your local recycling company and find out exactly what items they will take. Some places will take Styrofoam; others won't. Wash out any food containers before you place them in the bin. Remove paper wrappers from cans. Cardboard that has food stains or oils (for example, pizza boxes) can't be recycled. Yes, this takes longer than just dumping everything into a bin and letting someone else sort it out. That is the kind of attitude that has contributed to the state the world is in today.

No Lawns

Lawns, to put it mildly, are an environmental disaster. They rely on non-native grass species in most places and require huge amounts of water and chemicals to keep green. Movements like Food Not Lawns have sprung up over recent years, urging people to reconsider the time and effort they put into a crop that provides no actual benefit.

Replacing lawns with gardens might not be an option for everyone. Many municipalities and HOAs have rules requiring a lawn be maintained. Renters might not have a lot of control over their lawns either. That doesn't mean you have to dedicate yourself to keeping a green expanse. Evaluate your local ordinances, your rental agreement, and HOA rules to find out just how much lawn you have to

33. "10 Facts about Single-Use Plastic Bags," the Center for Biological Diversity, accessed April 30, 2020, https://www.biologicaldiversity.org/programs/population_and_sustainability/sustainability/plastic_bag_facts.html.

keep. Do these commandments pertain to both the front and back yard? What about the side areas of the house? Knowing the regulations is the first step in bending them to a more environmentally conscious arrangement.

If you can convert some of your lawn to garden space, plant native flowers, shrubs, and trees. They are already suited to the environment and won't require as much water and care, the bonus being that they will provide habitats and food for the native wildlife. If you can, let it go wild. Allowing the land to retake what was once forcibly cultivated gives room for the genius loci to settle.

If you live in a place without a yard, you can still keep potted native wildflowers on a porch or balcony. These may not have the same environmental impact, but they can serve as a way for you to connect to the land. They will also provide shelter to the genius loci who might find themselves surrounded on all sides by various man-made structures.

Keeping It Local, Keeping It Native

The plight of the honeybee has been another example of how environmental concerns can focus so narrowly that it misses the bigger picture. Honeybees and bumblebees are both suffering from diseases like colony collapse syndrome. However, they are just two of nearly 20,000 different bee species.[34] The focus on their struggles is due to them being domesticated and used in agriculture. They aren't the only pollinators, however, and all the other insects, birds, and bats that spread pollen are suffering their own

---

34. Troy Farah, "While We Worry about Honeybees, Other Pollinators Are Disappearing," *Discover* magazine, August 3, 2018, https://www.discovermagazine.com/environment/while-we-worry-about-honey bees-other-pollinators-are-disappearing.

threats due to habitat destruction, just to name one danger.[35] More good could be done by researching what local wildlife needs in order to flourish and do that. Build bee and insect hotels and stumperies to provide a home for all the insects that don't live in colonies. Erect bat houses. Set up a water station for butterflies. Like planting native plants, taking into account the needs of native pollinators strengthens the local ecology and shows respect to the land you are living on.

 EXERCISE
Connecting with the Genius Loci

Genius loci are spirits of the place. They can be tied to the land or to specific trees, rock outcroppings, bodies of water, and so on. Wherever you live, there will be spirits. They were there before you and will be there long after you are gone. Unless something has angered or annoyed them, you could go your entire life without having an interaction with the genius loci. If you are going to try to improve the local environment you live in, say by planting a garden or picking up trash, it can be helpful to know what they want. At the very least, it is polite and can avoid the aforementioned angering of local spirits.

Pick a spot outdoors, a tree, a potted plant, or some other natural feature. Settle next to it. Center and ground yourself. Now send out calming, peaceful, and welcoming energies. You want to broadcast your friendly energies. Visualize what it is that you want to accomplish; go through the steps you

---

35. "7 Things You Should Know about Bees and Other Pollinators," Smithsonian's National Zoo and Conservation Biology Institute, October 3, 2018, https://nationalzoo.si.edu/animals/news/7-things-you-should-know-about-bees-and-other-pollinators.

will take and what it will look like when you are finished. Taking the example of creating a garden, visualize the alterations you will make to the land, where you will dig, what plants you'll be planting, and how it will look once everything has been established and is in bloom. In effect, you are applying for a metaphysical building permit and informing whatever spirits that are around what it is you mean to do.

Once you've declared your intentions, wait for any response from the genius loci. If you have any feelings of dread, fear, or uneasiness, those are signs the local spirits don't approve of what you are doing. They might actively work against you by withering your plants, inviting animals to eat your vegetables, or make the ground so difficult to work that you give up at the digging stage. If, instead, you get feelings of happiness, joy, or excitement, that is a permission given to go ahead with the plan. These responses can also come in other forms: bad smells, indicating condemnation, or sweet smells, meaning you have their favor. You may even get no response, which can indicate that the spirits want to mull over your plans before giving their opinion. In that case you should end the exercise and try again a couple of days later.

If you get no response or mixed signals, you can also turn to divination to find out if your presence and plans are welcome or not. It could turn out that the genius loci don't care one way or another. They are not creatures that share human tastes and concerns, after all. It is, however, always better to ask permission than forgiveness.

Sustainable Offerings

When out foraging, it is often customary to make an offering to the plant or tree that you are taking from. Unfortunately, many of the traditional offerings end up causing harm. Coins have metals that can leach into the soil and harm plants and trees. Milk can curdle and encourage the growth of harmful fungus. Food can contain ingredients that can poison wildlife. Water, energy, birdseed, or the seeds of native plants can be substituted and are generally safe. The key is to not leave behind anything that will cause problems for the entities you are trying to thank.

Cultural Appropriation: What It Is and How Not to Do It

Let's get this out of the way at the start: appropriation is real. It happens. This is not up for debate. Also, appropriation does not equal appreciation.

When I was a baby witch, I felt a connection with the spirit of Turtle. For years I said Turtle was my totem animal (a concept I was introduced to by Jean M. Auel's *Earth's Children* series). As the years progressed, I came across the idea that claiming to have a totem as a white woman was offensive and appropriative. I wish I could write that I accepted this information gracefully and went about my business, never being problematic ever again. Alas, this wasn't so. I bristled at the idea that I "wasn't allowed" to use the concept. After years of feeling the outsider, of fighting against patriarchal control, I didn't like being told what I could or couldn't do with my spirituality.

Once I got past my anger, I moved on to bargaining. I dropped the term *totem* and adopted *spirit animal* under the misguided assumption that it was a generic phrase. Other cultures had animal spirits that people had relationships with and revered, I argued. I even at one point self-published a book under a pseudonym about mythical spirit guides. It was, as is indicated by the description, a book dedicated to finding one's "spirit guide" among various mythological creatures. As if that was a clever workaround to the actual issue of appropriation. I ended up removing the book from publication later.

But it increasingly didn't sit well with me. How does one uphold the tenet "Do no harm" and still use a term that actively hurts others? About this time, others were struggling with this and trying to come up with alternatives. They turned to fiction, specifically J. K. Rowling's Harry Potter series and its use of *patronus* and Phillip Pullman's His Dark Materials series and the term *dæmon*. Neither term worked for me. A patronus refers to a magically conjured creature used to fight off dementors (evil creatures in the series). Dæmons, in Pullman's books, were representations of people's souls. Neither term encapsulated what my relationship with Turtle was, nor did the terms *familiar, fetch, fylgja,* or others

I saw being offered up. I wanted to drop the offensive terms, but I didn't want to adopt ill-fitting ones. I felt stuck.

And then in 2017, I was reading *Clearing Spaces* by Khi Armand and came across the term *helping spirit*. Everything clicked for me. Turtle was a helping spirit. He aided me in my magick. He taught me lessons. He listened to my bitching. And, like Hestia, he stayed in the background those long years when I struggled, waiting for when I was ready to get to work again. Not a god, not a house sprite, not a creation of my magick, but a helper in spirit form who took on the image of a snapping turtle. This phrase *helping spirit* allowed me to identify my relationship with Turtle and not at the expense of indigenous people.

There are three lessons to take away from my experience:

1. When you feel that automatic rejection and anger at being told you are being appropriative, stop and acknowledge that emotion and use it as a warning Klaxon that you are in the wrong. There is a saying, "When you're accustomed to privilege, equality feels like oppression." The corollary here is that when you are used to everything being open to you, being denied feels like oppression. Take a moment and sit with that feeling of rebellion. Thank it for bringing your attention to your privilege. And then, once you have acknowledged that, move on to the next lesson.

2. Terms and concepts are not interchangeable or generic. The word *totem* is Ojibwe. *Spirit animal* is a concept used by Anishinaabe and other indigenous tribes.[36] Both have very specific religious meanings that don't translate to Western spiritual experiences in the same way that the Eucharist is

36. Mari (@wordglass), Twitter thread, February 4, 2018, 11:56 a.m., https://twitter.com/wordglass/status/960210356629995523.

not analogous to a Baptist communion or the Wiccan cakes and ale. Beyond that, however, is the fact that one has to be part of the tribe that the concepts of spirit animals and totems belong to in order to have them. In the United States of America, for example, membership into a native tribe is not just a matter of blood, but also of being registered and recognized as a member. After centuries of genocide, colonization, and oppression, it is understandable that indigenous groups would make an effort to maintain and preserve their culture through various means. The idea of certain religious objects or rituals being only for use by adherents is not new or unusual. No one outside the Jewish faith would wear a yarmulke, nor would a non-Muslim use a prayer rug. And even if they did, those items wouldn't have the meaning inherent to them when being used by people outside of the faiths they belong to. While there has been a lot of "borrowing" in early and contemporary Wiccan and Pagan practices, it's time to stop that and actively shed what was taken from other, oppressed cultures. Yes, this means dropping the idea of being an "eclectic" witch who collects practices like a magpie. It means dropping the word *gypsy* from our vocabulary because we acknowledge that it is a slur. It means recognizing that karma is not equivalent to the concept of the threefold law. It means—

3. Deconstructing our Pagan and witchcraft practices is the best way to move forward. I have joked before that my family sprouted from corn nuts strewn across the Great Plains. My family didn't really talk about our history or where our ancestors came from. I grew up in the middle of Wyoming, where culture was *Monday Night Football* and "Achy Breaky

Heart." I was raised Baptist. And so when I first started learning about Paganism and witchcraft, I was immediately drawn to "Native American" practices. Of course, these practices were taught and run by white people who couldn't explain which Native Americans the practices came from. It wasn't until a few years ago when my sister did a DNA test and found Irish and Scottish roots in our genes that I've been looking at witchcraft traditions from those cultures. Where does that leave me with regard to Hestia? Greek mythology, deities, and rituals come from open practices, so I can still work with her without causing harm. With Turtle I had to interrogate how I defined our relationship unflinchingly, but I couldn't do that until I had stopped trying to skirt responsibility for participating in cultural appropriation. You will have to do the same. You will have to read widely, listen to minority peoples, and investigate everything you believe. As witches, we know that words have power. You will have to make sure those you use are available to you in the first place.

Witchcraft and Paganism have been going through a reckoning during the twenty-first century. After generations of watching their cultures and heritages plundered by white people, many BIPOC are calling out the appropriation.

EXERCISE
Spot the Cultural Appropriation

Pick one of the topics on the following list and research its origins and how it is relevant to the subject of cultural appropriation: smudging, palo santo and white sage, dream catchers, dreadlocks, yoga, chakras, karma, or abalone shell.

Closed versus Open Practices

With the increased awareness of cultural appropriation with regard to Paganism and witchcraft comes the concept of closed and open practices. Closed practices are those that require membership or initiation. Those within the practice are the ones who determine whether someone is part of the practice. Oftentimes, practices are closed to safeguard knowledge, rites, or mysteries. They can also be closed as a defensive measure against appropriation. Open practices, on the other hand, do not require initiation or membership.

This shouldn't be a controversial concept, and yet there are people who will rail against the idea that anything can be denied them. The point is made worse by the fact that early Wicca, witchcraft, occult, and Pagan practitioners stole concepts from marginalized cultures, filed off the serial numbers, and presented the ideas as their own. It wasn't right then and it isn't right now. And so there are certain concepts, terms, and practices that have been taught for decades as being Pagan that have their origins in closed practices that many people might not even be aware have been appropriated because of that distortion.

It is important for witches and Pagans, especially white witches and Pagans, to be aware of this distinction. If you are invited into a closed practice by a practitioner, treat it as the sacred honor it is and respect the closed aspects. Do not reveal what you have learned—that was a gift to you and you alone. Also, be aware that religions and practices aren't homogeneous or monolithic. Just because one person or group has invited you into their circle doesn't mean everyone who is a part of that circle will also welcome you. If you are not part of the group, do not speak over others as if you have authority. All of this really boils down to treating others with respect.

We also have the responsibility to investigate the origins of any activity we bring into our practice. There is a world of information on the internet to aid in research. This is no different from studying the magickal properties of plants or the correspondences of the elements or the movement of the stars. Witchcraft has always been about exerting one's will on the world. That will, applied without sufficient knowledge, will at best simply not manifest or at worst will cause harm.

Supporting Indigenous Practitioners

In 2015 European clothing designer Kokon To Zai released a sweater that copied the design of a Nunavut parka. The original design was meant to be protective and had been made by a Nunavut man in the 1920s.[37] This is not an isolated incident. Fashion has an extensive legacy of stealing designs from indigenous peoples and cultures. More often than not their victims can't do anything about it. Thanks to centuries of colonization, racism, and systemic oppression, they don't have the resources to take on a well-funded fashion house. The fashion industry then just moves on to a new conquest in the next season.

One way we, and by "we" I mean white Pagans and witches, can help redress this continuing injustice is to be mindful of our purchases. Many items can be bought from indigenous artists. You can skip Target and instead look for jewelry, art, and artifacts from

37. "Nunavut Family Outraged after Fashion Label Copies Sacred Inuit Design," CBC Radio, November 27, 2015, https://www.cbc.ca/radio/asithappens /as-it-happens-wednesday-edition-1.3336554/nunavut-family-outraged-after -fashion-label-copies-sacred-inuit-design-1.3336560.

actual BIPOC. If they are making items for sale, then it is proper for you to buy it. Not only will you be supporting a small business, but you will get something with a connection to the culture which is an order of magnitude more meaningful than a mass-produced trinket sold through Walmart.

No Ethical Consumption under Capitalism

At the end of 2019 Bree Newsome Bass took on the concept of being a capitalist on Twitter. Her tweets read in part:

> I don't know who needs to hear this but you are not a cap-
> italist. You are a salaried employee working in an industry
> owned by an actual capitalist. People keep confusing simple
> commerce—which has always existed—with capitalism, a
> specific type of economy. …
>
> Folks swear up and down they are capitalists and don't
> actually own anything. The people who have the power to
> repossess your belongings if you miss a payment are the
> true capitalist. You are a worker and a consumer trying to
> be in false class solidarity [with] billionaires.[38]

At a time when economic inequality is reaching new heights, seeing capitalism separated out from commerce is an important distinction. Understanding the difference is needed when discussing anti-capitalism.

When I first conceived the idea that capitalism is incompatible with Paganism and witchcraft, I kept it to myself. Anyone who complained about capitalism and its side effects—its lack of a living wage, exploitation of vulnerable populations, global

---

38. Bree Newsome Bass (@BreeNewsome), Twitter thread, December 12, 2019, 8:04 a.m., https://twitter.com/BreeNewsome/status/1205126175372271617.

warming—were often considered lazy individuals who didn't con-
tribute and refused to pull themselves up by their bootstraps. The
common retort I would see on social media aimed at anyone who
brought up the problems with capitalism was "I see you hate capitalism and yet you work at a fast food restaurant—interesting."
The point seemingly being that people participating in a capitalist
system have no standing to complain about it. That logic, however,
isn't as infallible as people would think. It is more along the lines of
telling serfs in medieval Europe that their "participation" in feudal
systems means they can't advocate for its abolishment.

Capitalism is set up to extract as much value out of everything—materials, natural resources, even people—as possible.
There is no end goal, just the ever-continuing quest to make more
profits this quarter than the previous. Workers, those who provide
the labor extracting that value, are told that they will flourish and
thrive as the economy does. And it is true that at the beginning
many people did so. However, as time has gone on, worker wages
have stagnated as the salaries of CEOs have soared. Chemicals
from factories are dumped into rivers because the fines for that
crime are less than what it would cost to deal with the waste in a
responsible way. Unions, which allow people to work together for
the benefit of all members, are opposed—sometimes violently—
because collective bargaining can mean less profit. Corporations,
by design, are creatures that are always hungry, gobbling up whatever they can, and are never sated. What it boils down to, for me, is
that a system in which a small few profit from the labor of others
without sharing that profit with them is a system that shouldn't
be. As an earth-centered belief system, Paganism cannot ally itself
with an economic system that views the world as a resource to
exploit. Witchcraft has always been a tool for the dispossessed
against the powerful, the complete opposite of corporations.

When I was working on this book, the world was experiencing the COVID-19 pandemic. In the US we saw massive unemployment and the tanking of our economy. Facebook groups popped up so neighbors could coordinate food pickups. Hundreds of sewists started churning out cloth masks for friends and strangers. Corporations were not taking care of people—communities were.

This is not, however, me saying that Pagans and witches shouldn't participate in commerce. They've done so for centuries before Ford and Carnegie came on the scene. Many witches served as local wisewomen and wisemen who helped people with various issues. Before capitalism, people grew crops, raised livestock, made crafts, raised fences, cobbled shoes, and dug ditches as livelihoods that involved not only coin but barter. Even in a capitalist society you have housewives raising chickens or taking on piecework for "pin money." Today we see countless people turning their passions and hobbies into side hustles.

It could be easy to overlook Hestia and the home when it comes to not only capitalism but commerce. The goddess of the senate she may be, but Hestia isn't involved in the marketplace. And the home can be viewed as the result of our consumption. We work to make money to buy things to put in our homes, the same homes we rarely spend time in because we have to work more hours to afford all the things we filled our house with. Then again, put that way, you might see how the Hestia-home relationship connects to our capitalist society.

In all this thinking and connecting and relating, however, we hit a difficulty. As stated, we can't opt out of our capitalist society. We have rent or mortgages to pay. Water, electricity, gas, internet, and other utilities aren't free. Change, radical and deliberate change, is required to shift our societies to a more equitable system. That realization can often lead one to throw up their hands in defeat. If you can't beat them, after all, why not join them?

So how do we, as Pagans and witches, navigate a system that is antithetical to our morals, beliefs, and being? As my friend Lawerence once said, "There has never been ethical consumption. That's why we respect the kill." To eat meat, an animal has to die. To eat plants and vegetables, the land must be disturbed. Foraging takes from other animals, pollinators, and people. Widen our view and we see that to wear clothes we have to buy from retailers who might use sweatshop labor. If we try to avoid that by making our own clothes, we still have to buy the fabric that was produced by processes that pollute. To communicate with our friends and loved ones we use technology that uses minerals torn from the earth and put together in unsafe working conditions. The point is not to move into caves in the mountains and wear robes made from woven grass. We have to accept that consumption is destruction, and that our goal is not the elimination of that destruction, but to eliminate unnecessary and egregious harm. We want ethical and sustainable farming practices, living wages, and renewable energy resources.

No change ever comes without struggle. And as empty and destructive as capitalism is, it has proven to be responsive to the threats to its diet. Starving the beast of your time, attention, and money can hurt it. This means being conscious of where you are putting your dollars. It means paying attention to where the things you buy come from. It may mean spending more on local or ethical items. It may also mean going without rather than giving your resources, or energy, to companies that put profit over all.

I touch upon this briefly in chapter 10 when I discuss making your own cleaning supplies and also in this chapter in Exercise 1: Shopping. The importance of the home as a crucible for change cannot be overstated. We can reduce or eliminate unfettered consumption when it comes to our homes. We can learn to repair appliances and furniture rather than buying new ones. We can limit our use of electricity and water. All these activities help us create, in our homes, the environment we want to see in our larger society. As above, so below.

Finally, we must recognize that there is no ethical consumption in capitalism. Every transaction is a trade that affects someone somewhere: the clothes sewn by workers in India, the chocolate made from cocoa beans picked by child labor in Ivory Coast, the new cell phone that includes coltan from Central Africa.[39] We may not be bringing down a deer with bow and arrow or harvesting grain for our bread, but we aren't exempt from the destruction that is inherent in all consumption.

As individuals, we can take steps to mitigate our culpability in capitalism. However, it is corporations that are the chief antagonist, producing most of the pollution, leveraging their money to interfere in local politics, and more. It is on us, as Pagans and as witches, to not only shop local and recycle, but also vote for and support governments and politicians who can make societal change. We have to be loud, attend rallies and protests, and bend

39. Rebecca Ratcliffe, "Major Western Brands Pay Indian Garment Workers 11p an Hour," *Guardian*, February 1, 2019, https://www.theguardian.com/global-development/2019/feb/01/major-western-brands-pay-indian-garment-workers-11p-an-hour; Peter Whoriskey and Rachel Siegel, "Cocoa's Child Laborers," *Washington Post*, June 5, 2019, https://www.washingtonpost.com/graphics/2019/business/hershey-nestle-mars-chocolate-child-labor-west-africa/; David Love, "The Mining of Coltan: Chances Are Your Smartphone Was Manufactured with African Blood,s" *Atlanta Black Star*, September 25, 2017, https://atlantablackstar.com/2017/09/25/mining-coltan-chances-smartphone-manufactured-african-blood/.

capitalism to our wills through financial and other support to politicians who can make social change. For some people this is an uncomfortable challenge. And yet it is necessary.

Hestia is an original status quo breaker. She didn't accept the norms of marriage but told the leader of the gods she wouldn't be marrying. That earned her not only her place as the goddess in charge of the most important position on Olympus, but also the standing as the most important goddess to the state. She shows us that we can, and are obligated to, advocate for ourselves and that we can make change. We can become the underpinnings of society.

EXERCISE 1
Shopping

Make a list of various necessities and things you buy regularly and research any local distributors you can buy from instead of corporations. Identify things you can make (soup stock or tomato sauce, for example) and research recipes.

Look into plants—herbs, fruits, or vegetables—you can grow to become a little more self-sufficient. Research community gardens or local groups that trade produce.

Take one item you buy regularly. Research it thoroughly. What company makes it? Who do they employ? Where do the raw materials come from? Are there any ethical or social problems with the company or the product they produce?

EXERCISE 2
Politics

National government offices are important, but so are local politics. Research your local city, county, and state government officials. If your area elects judges, find out who they are and see if they have ruled in ways that are just. Who is on your city councils? School boards? What are their politics, and what do they think their jobs are supposed to be? Do you know when your city council meets? Have you ever attended one? Yes, you are going to have to get involved in some way. Take some time to inform yourself of the local politics and make goals that are reasonable for you to engage civically. Remember, Hestia wasn't just the goddess of the hearth. She was the goddess of the state as well.

🌿 EXERCISE 3
Ecology

Research the history and ecology of the area you live in. Who were the people who originally lived there? How did they live? What did they grow? What animals did they raise? Who did they trade with? What did they eat? This will help you to identify crops that are native and grow easily in your area. What happened to the people? Many indigenous peoples, especially in the Americas, were displaced and colonized, but they still exist. Are there any organizations or charities that aid those communities? Can you give to them?

Now what about the present day? What is the main employer in your area? What is the dominant industry? Is it ethical? Is there a union or an attempt to build a union? What is the main export? Import? What percentage of the population is unemployed, underemployed, or homeless? What social services or charities are there that help?

All these exercises are meant to help you forge a greater relationship with your community. Just because corporations seem to hold all the cards doesn't mean the individual is powerless. Short of revolution (which I am not discounting), capitalism can be influenced. After all, it depends on the coerced labor and money of the masses to survive. People have more power than they are credited with. And as witches and Pagans, we shouldn't overlook any avenue or outlet of power available to us.

CONCLUSION

Maxims about the home abound. The home is where we hang our hats, where our hearts are. The home is sweet and there is no place like it. Home, we're told, is more than just the house; it is not constrained by bricks and boards and shingles. Around the world, across various cultures, and throughout history, home has had an ever-changing definition. Understanding this can bring about a sense of freedom, of being uncoupled from expectations. Home can be what we make of it. With that freedom can come uncertainty as well. When faced with infinite options, how do we choose? For me, Hestia provided the girder on which to build my definition of hearth and home.

Writing *The Scent of Lemon & Rosemary* has been a labor of love in service to Hestia. The goal is not to proselytize but more to raise her profile in a world that needs a bit of comfort and stability. It has also been an act of worship, refining my relationship with Hestia. I hope that you gained as much from this book as I did from writing it.

Take care. Stay safe. And blessed be.

Appendix
INGREDIENT CORRESPONDENCES

This is a quick list of a selection of ingredients that you can reference when putting together any culinary magick. Each entry includes the element it is associated with (if applicable) and a short list of magickal properties.

Almonds: Air | Mental clarity, money, prosperity, wisdom

Apples, Apple Juice, Applesauce: Water | Healing, Love

Baking Soda: Activating other spell components, increasing success, speeding up the timeline of spell goals

Basil: Fire | Love, money, protection

Bay Leaves: Fire | Healing, protection, strength

Carrot: Fire | Healing, fertility, lust

Cashew: Fire | Communication, love, money

Celery: Fire | Lust, mental powers, peace, serenity

Cinnamon: Fire | Healing, love, power, success,

Clove: Fire | Love, money, protection

Egg: Fertility, abundance

Flaxseed Egg: Fire | Money

Garlic: Fire | Healing, protection

Ginger: Fire | Money, power, success

Honey: Fire | Enhancing the effectiveness of spells

Lemon: Water | Purification, love, blessings, enhancing the magick of spellwork

Maple Syrup: Air | Love, money

Oats: Earth | Money

Olive Oil: Fire | Peace, protection, healing, inviting the Divine into your spellwork

Onion: Fire | Healing, money, protection, revealing ulterior motives or hidden information

Peanuts: Earth | Stability, manifesting your magickal intentions

Pistachios: Air | Breaking a love spell (because of this, do not use in recipes meant to inspire or increase love), curse breaking

Potato: Earth | Healing, seeing beyond the surface

Rosemary: Fire | Protection, love, mental powers, purification, healing, sleep

Salt: Earth | Protection, purification

Spinach: Earth | Fertility, prosperity

Sugar: Happiness, used to attract energies

Thyme: Water | Healing, sleep, psychic powers, love, purification, courage

Vanilla, Vanilla Extract: Water | Love, mental powers

Walnuts: Fire | Health, mental powers, prosperity

Wheat: Earth | Fertility, money

Yeast: To support growth, transformation

BIBLIOGRAPHY

Aeschines. *The Speeches of Aeschines*. Translated by Charles Darwin Adams. Cambridge, MA: Harvard University Press, 1919.

Alech, Alice, and Cécile Le Galliard. *The 7 Wonders of Olive Oil*. New York: Familius, 2017.

Armand, Khi. *Clearing Spaces*. New York: Sterling Ethos, 2017.

Bloom, Jessi. *Creating Sanctuary*. Portland, OR: Timber Press, 2018.

Bolen, Jean Shinoda. *Goddesses in Older Women*. New York: Harper Perennial, 2001.

Cunningham, Scott. *Cunningham's Encyclopedia of Crystal, Gem and Metal Magic*. St. Paul, MN: Llewellyn Publications, 2002.

Cunningham, Scott. *Cunningham's Encyclopedia of Magical Herbs*. St. Paul, MN: Llewellyn Publications, 1985.

De Clercq, Ina. *DIY Beauty*. New York: Adams Media, 2019.

Dunwich, Gerina. *Herbal Magick*. Newburyport, MA: Weiser Books, 2002.

Farah, Troy. "While We Worry about Honeybees, Other Pollinators Are Disappearing." *Discover Magazine*, August 3, 2018. https://www.discovermagazine.com/environment/while-we-worry-about-honeybees-other-pollinators-are-disappearing.

France, Peter. *Hermits: The Insights of Solitude*. New York: St. Martin's, 1997.

Galper, Amy, and Christina Daigneault. *Plant-Powered Beauty*. Dallas, TX: BenBella Books, 2018.

Gattefossé, René-Maurice. *Gattefossé's Aromatherapy*. Translated by C. W. Daniel Company. Essex, England: C. W. Daniel Company, 1993.

Gillotte, Galen. *Sacred Stones of the Goddess*. St. Paul, MN: Llewellyn Publications, 2003.

Green, Marian. *A Witch Alone*. Charlottesville, VA: Hampton Roads, 2009.

Griffin, Paul. "CDP Carbon Majors Report 2017." The Carbon Majors Database, July 2017. https://b8f65cb373b1b7b15feb-c70d8ead6ced550b4d987d7c03fcdd1d.ssl.cf3.rackcdn.com/cms/reports/documents/000/002/327/original/Carbon-Majors-Report-2017.pdf?1499691240.

Habbach, Hajar, Kathryn Hampton, and Ranit Mishori. "You Will Never See Your Child Again: The Persistent Psychological Effects of Family Separation." Physicians for Human Rights. February 25, 2020. https://phr.org/our-work/resources/you-will-never-see-your-child-again-the-persistent-psychological-effects-of-family-separation/.

Hayes, Shannon. *Radical Housekeeping*. Richmondville, NY: Left to Write Press, 2010.

Hill, Melissa. "Imbolc Invocation to the Fire Goddesses." *Patheos* (blog). January 21, 2020. https://www.patheos.com/blogs/dandelionlady/2020/01/imbolc-invocation-to-the-fire-goddesses.html.

Hesiod, the Homeric Hymns, and Homerica. Translated by Hugh G. Evelyn-White. Cambridge, MA: Harvard University Press, 1914.

Kondo, Marie. *The Life-Changing Magic of Tidying Up.* Berkeley, CA: Ten Speed Press, 2014.

Liu, Yong, Anne G. Wheaton, Daniel P. Chapman, Timothy J. Cunningham, Hua Lu, and Janet B. Croft. "Prevalence of Healthy Sleep Duration among Adults—United States, 2014." *Morbidity and Mortality Weekly Report* 65, no. 6 (February 19, 2016): 137–41. http://dx.doi.org/10.15585/mmwr.mm6506a1.

Lizzo. "Tiny Desk Concert." *NPR* video, 16:59, July 29, 2019. https://www.npr.org/2019/07/29/732097345/lizzo-tiny-desk-concert.

Llewellyn, Aine. "Breath, the Foundational Practice." *Patheos* (blog), January 24, 2020. https://www.patheos.com/blogs/ainellewellyn/2020/01/b-for-breath/.

Love, David. "The Mining of Coltan: Chances Are Your Smartphone Was Manufactured with African Blood." *Atlanta Black Star*, September 25, 2017. https://atlantablackstar.com/2017/09/25/mining-coltan-chances-smartphone-manufactured-african-blood/.

Maker, Melissa. *Clean My Space.* Toronto: Viking Canada, 2017.

Mari (@wordglass). Twitter thread, February 4, 2018, 11:56 a.m. https://twitter.com/wordglass/status/960210356629995523.

Matsumoto, Shoukei. *A Monk's Guide to a Clean House and Mind.* Translated by Ian Samhammer. London: Penguin Books, 2018.

Mendelson, Cheryl. *Laundry.* New York: Scribner, 1999.

Miernowska, Marysia. *The Witch's Herbal Apothecary.* Beverly, MA: Quarto, 2020.

Nellis, Ashley. "The Color of Justice: Racial and Ethnic Disparity in State Prisons." The Sentencing Project. June 14, 2016. https://www.sentencingproject.org/publications/color-of-justice-racial-and-ethnic-disparity-in-state-prisons/.

Newsome Bass, Bree (@BreeNewsome). Twitter thread, December 12, 2019, 8:04 a.m. https://twitter.com/BreeNewsome/status/1205126175372271617.

"Nunavut Family Outraged after Fashion Label Copies Sacred Inuit Design." CBC Radio, November 27, 2015. https://www.cbc.ca/radio/asithappens/as-it-happens-wednesday-edition-1.3336554/nunavut-family-outraged-after-fashion-label-copies-sacred-inuit-design-1.3336560.

Ovid. *Fasti.* Translated by A. J. Boyle and R. D. Woodard. New York: Penguin, 2000.

Pindar. *Nemean Odes.* Translated by Diane Arnson Svarlien. Perseus Digital Library, 1990. http://www.perseus.tufts.edu/hopper/text?doc=Perseus%3Atext%3A1999.01.0162%3Abook%3DN.%3Apoem%3D11.

Ratcliffe, Rebecca. "Major Western Brands Pay Indian Garment Workers 11p an Hour." *Guardian*, February 1, 2019. https://www.theguardian.com/global-development/2019/feb/01/major-western-brands-pay-indian-garment-workers-11p-an-hour.

Robyn, Kathryn L. *Spiritual Housecleaning.* Oakland, CA: New Harbinger Publications, 2001.

"7 Things You Should Know about Bees and Other Pollinators." Smithsonian's National Zoo and Conservation Biology Institute. October 3, 2018. https://nationalzoo.si.edu/animals/news/7-things-you-should-know-about-bees-and-other-pollinators.

Schoff, Jill Potvin. *Green Clean*. Mount Joy, PA: Creative Home-owner, 2019.

"10 Facts about Single-Use Plastic Bags." The Center for Biological Diversity. Accessed April 30, 2020. https://www.biological diversity.org/programs/population_and_sustainability /sustainability/plastic_bag_facts.html.

Thompson, Patricia J. "Hestian Hermeneutics: A Lens of Analysis for Home Economics." In *The Conversation and Company of Educated Women*. Edited by Linda Peterat. Champaign, IL: University of Illinois, 1986.

Whoriskey, Peter, and Rachel Siegel. "Cocoa's Child Laborers." *Washington Post*, June 5, 2019. https://www.washingtonpost .com/graphics/2019/business/hershey-nestle-mars-chocolate -child-labor-west-africa/.

Wiking, Meik. *The Little Book of Hygge*. New York: William Morrow, 2017.

Wolverton, B. C., Willard L. Douglas, and Keith Bounds. "A Study of Interior Landscape Plants for Indoor Air Pollution Abatement." NASA, July 1989.

Zaslavsky, Claudia. "Women as the First Mathematicians." *International Study Group on Ethnomathematics Newsletter* 7, no. 1 (January 1992): n.p. https://web.nmsu.edu/~pscott/isgem71 .htm.

ACKNOWLEDGMENTS

This book would not have been possible without the support of my husband, Stephan Kelly. He took over nearly all the household chores—laundry, cooking, dishes—and helped our children with their remote learning, all so I could concentrate on writing. Thank you, love.

My children, Charlotte and Benjamin, were equally supportive and understanding of all the time I had to spend away from them.

Thank you to my editors, Elysia Gallo and Lauryn Heineman. Both worked hard to help me make this book what it is.

My great thanks to Hamid Khan and David Zoltan, who answered my questions at late hours.

Thank you as well to Lawerence Hawkins, for the concept of "respecting the kill" with regard to capitalism. That one musing shaped much of what I wrote about the subject.

Thanks be to Dionysus, as a great volume of wine was consumed while I wrote. On a related note, many apologies to my liver—your service is appreciated.

Finally, no thanks go to the cats, Jake and Barley. Their constant insistence on attention and pets severely hampered my writing speed.

To Write to the Author

If you wish to contact the author or would like more information about this book, please write to the author in care of Llewellyn Worldwide Ltd. and we will forward your request. Both the author and the publisher appreciate hearing from you and learning of your enjoyment of this book and how it has helped you. Llewellyn Worldwide Ltd. cannot guarantee that every letter written to the author can be answered, but all will be forwarded. Please write to:

Raechel Henderson
℅ Llewellyn Worldwide
2143 Wooddale Drive
Woodbury, MN 55125-2989

Please enclose a self-addressed stamped envelope for reply,
or $1.00 to cover costs. If outside the U.S.A., enclose
an international postal reply coupon.

Many of Llewellyn's authors have websites with additional nformation and resources. For more information, please visit our website at http://www.llewellyn.com.

Notes

Notes

Notes

Notes

Notes